PERFECT BUSINESS PLAN

Ron Johnson, an independent consultant since 1980, spends his time helping people to plan and to manage change, dealing with the operational, business and 'people' aspects of the organization. He is equally at home with the directors of large corporations, sole traders or senior officials in public service. Over the years his work has included running workshops for would-be entrepreneurs on the practical problems of setting up a business. He has also conducted workshops for directors and managers on business planning, budget preparation and managing change, gearing these closely to company needs.

Ron Johnson is a prolific writer and frequent public speaker whose books include *How to Manage People* (Hutchinson, 1984), *Building Success through People* (Random House Business Books, 1986), *Perfect Teamwork* (Arrow Books, 1995), *The 24-Hour Business Plan* (Third edition, 2000), *The Art of Empowerment* (FT Pitman, 1998, co-author David Redmond) and *Diversity Incorporated* (FT Prentice Hall, 2000, co-author David Redmond).

The book reflects his wide experience in helping people come to grips with the business planning process and tackling the everyday challenges of surviving and succeeding. He is a Companion of the Chartered Institute of Personnel and Development and an active member of the Federation of Small Businesses.

OTHER TITLES IN THE SERIES

PERFECT
BUSINESS PLAN

All you need to get it right first time

Ron Johnson

RANDOM HOUSE

BUSINESS BOOKS

This edition published by Random House Business Books in 2003

7 9 10 8 6

Copyright © 1993, 2003 by Ron Johnson

First published in the United Kingdom by Century Business in 1993.

Random House Business Books
The Random House Group Limited
20 Vauxhall Bridge Road, London, SW1V 2SA

Random House Australia (Pty) Limited
20 Alfred Street, Milsons Point, Sydney,
New South Wales 2061, Australia

Random House New Zealand Limited
18 Poland Road, Glenfield
Auckland 10, New Zealand

Random House (Pty) Limited
Endulini, 5a Jubilee Road, Parktown 2193, South Africa

The Random House Group Limited Reg. No. 954009

www.randomhouse.co.uk

businessbooks@randomhouse.co.uk

A CIP catalogue record for this book
is available from the British Library

Papers used by Random House
are natural, recyclable products made from wood grown in
sustainable forests. The manufacturing processes conform to
the environmental regulations of the country of origin

ISBN 0 8441 3148 3

Typeset in Sabon by SX Composing DTP, Rayleigh, Essex
Printed and bound in Great Britain by
Bookmarque Ltd, Croydon, Surrey

Contents

FOREWORD

Since the first edition several business factors have changed. The Internet, often coupled with other forms of digital technology, is now an integral tool of almost every business. There has also been an explosion of interest in health, safety and environmental concerns and related legislation that impacts on businesses in major ways. Entrepreneurs are now finding that public bodies and charitable trusts are prepared to offer grants, for example to encourage employment generation or the introduction of new technology. Any entrepreneur who applies for such grants will need to take this into account in drawing up or revizing business plans.

Virtually every company that does business today has to deal with a diversity of people – as customers, suppliers, business partners or employees. In many parts of the world people are no longer willing to be treated unfairly because they are women, or because they have some other distinguishing feature – be it race, nationality, creed, background, personality, sexual orientation, life-style, age or disability. In many countries there is legislation, for example in Australia, Europe, Singapore, South Africa and the United States, covering equality of opportunity in relation to gender, race, disability and age. It makes sound business sense to take full account of this diversity in the way you conduct your operation.

This text has been fully revised to take account of these developments.

SECTION TITLES

PART I – HOW TO USE THIS BOOK
1. Planning and learning.
2. The importance of research.
3. Decisions and their financial implications.
4. Implications of the Internet and digital technology.
5. Keeping abreast of change.

PART II – PLANNING TO PLAN
6. The purpose of planning.
7. Study the outline business plan.
8. Set out your planning timetable.
9. Outline the business you want to establish or develop.
10. Start to collect the basic information you will need.
11. Make some tentative decisions.
12. Sketch out your financial strategy.
13. Identify the key decision makers.
14. List the requirements of the decision makers.

PART III – ESSENTIAL EXPERTISE
15. List the people who will help you draw up the plan.
16. Check the expertise you need.
17. Secure accountancy advice, especially taxation matters.
18. Secure marketing advice or services.
19. Secure sales advice.
20. Secure advertizing advice or services.
21. Secure exporting or importing advice and services.
22. Secure advice on form of business.
23. Secure insurance advice and services.
24. Consider interpretation and translation services.
25. Secure legal advice and services.
26. Consider advice and services on patents, copyright, trade and service marks.
27. Secure advice and/or services on property matters and location.

PART V – BASIC ESTIMATES

56. Position your products and services.
57. Revise pricing structure.
58. Prepare basic estimates on costs, price and profit.
59. Estimate the business risks involved.
60. Review your pricing structure.
61. Draw up a specification for your location and premises.
62. Set out your sales forecasts and sales targets.
63. Forecast your sales revenue.
64. Firm up your advertizing strategy.
65. Describe how you will convert these responses into sales.
66. Prepare your credit control for sales.

PART VI – ESSENTIAL CALCULATIONS

67. Estimate capital expenditure costs.
68. Calculate depreciation on capital items.
69. Estimate fixed costs.
70. Estimate variable costs.
71. Estimating wages and salaries.
72. Estimating telecommunications and postage costs.
73. Rent, business and water rates.
74. Estimate insurance costs.
75. Interest and loan repayments.
76. Vehicle and travel costs.
77. Depreciation.
78. List the sources of finance available.
79. Plan your capital investment strategy.
80. Revise your profit forecast.
81. Decide on how much stock to hold.
82. Forecast cash receipts and payments.
83. Work out the cash flow forecast.
84. Review your profit forecasts.
85. Prepare balance sheets.

LIST OF FIGURES IN MAIN TEXT

PART I

How to use this book

- Learn as you plan the business.
- Do your research.
- Be systematic in decision-making.
- Consider the Internet.
- Keep abreast of change.

1. Planning and Learning.
This book is addressed primarily to the manager of a small to medium-sized firm where the person in charge may be working alone or have just one or two partners, co-directors or other colleagues in the business.

Writing a plan is about making better decisions today – not about making tomorrow's decisions. Perhaps the most valuable part of the work involved in preparing the plan is not the finished plan itself – useful though that is. The best part is what you learn as you work through each part of the process, and the way in which this prepares you to make better decisions as the situation changes – because you understand how your business is related to the outside (to customers, suppliers and the business environment), and you know how each part fits together.

Topics that need to be re-visited are spelt out in the

1

text on each occasion, often with different emphases. This is so that you do not have to hunt for the information you require as you prepare your plan.

2. The Importance of Research.

Writing a business plan is NOT straightforward. You can't just start at page one and write it all out. It is tempting to take one's business idea at face value, but often this is a mistake. You need to take the idea apart, to see, in detail how it will work, and how you will secure sales and income.

If you already know a very great deal about your business, your customers, suppliers, competitors and the business environment, and how much you can sell at what price, and what each and every part of your business will cost, you will find you can skip quickly through the early sections of the book. I do not recommend this. Anyone who has studied the success and failures of new businesses or of enterprises that are embarking on new ventures or experiencing difficulties will tell you that one of the key factors in achieving success is 'research' – in other words your study of the marketplace and each and every facet of the business.

3. Decisions and their financial implications.

This book has been written for people who do not want to cut corners, but who do want the process explained in a straightforward way. The method to use is simple. Start at the beginning and work your way carefully through each step.

There are an enormous number of important decisions to take – and they all have a financial impact to a greater or lesser extent. Many of these decisions are inter-related. Change one decision and it changes many other figures in the financial estimates.

There are times when the text appears to repeat itself. In the early sections you are asked to do some sums in a quick approximate way and to draft parts of the text for your plan out in rough to begin with. As you do more work on the plan these sums must be repeated, but more accurately in the light of some decisions you have tentatively made and as more information becomes available. Your early drafts must also be reviewed as the pattern of your business unfolds.

You cannot do everything at once. You must decide in what order to make your decisions and do your sums. Whatever order you choose you will find you have to go back over previous work. There are a number of different orders in which you can tackle the various sections of the plan. Some methods are better than others: the order given in this text works.

4. Implications of the Internet and digital technology.

Over recent years there has been an enormous increase in the power of information technology and the amount of accessible information. What use can you make of this new tool? The Internet can be the central focus of your business or a tool to be used, for example, to gather information, for training, communications, purchasing, marketing, selling or recruitment. But this technology can bring risks as well as advantages. You will need to consider security – for example, virus protection, routine back-ups and possibly power supply protection and disaster recovery. You will need to decide who can use the Internet and how, bearing in mind possible misuses.

The Internet is one aspect of digital technology. Visual images can be readily digitized and computers with enormous power can be minute in size. Data, sound and visual images that can be conveyed over the Internet may actually be the product that you are selling to the customer. Much of the information you need to build up a credible business plan can be obtained on the Internet – for example about competitors, their products, services and prices; about customers, their needs, wants and buying habits; about property, suppliers and the availability of goods and services; about changes in legislation or the rules that govern your business or developments in the science and/or technology that your business employs.

A major advantage of the Internet is the way it enables you to contact people quickly. The speed at which detailed data can be transmitted by e-mail can be valuable. Who will require e-mail access in your company? How many e-mail addresses will that involve? Will you have any rules governing the use of e-mails? Will you have a web site? How will your customers find it? Will you expect the web site to promote your products and services? Will customers be able to buy your products online, or interact with your people to solve problems? Will you maintain the web site on a regular basis? Digital tools can also be used to link together key people into virtual teams across departments and in different locations. If you need specialist staff it could make sense for you to use the Internet – especially if you want people who can use it! The range of jobs advertised is very wide, and the medium appeals particularly to professional people.

Be selective and don't be afraid to take a phased approach, making a start by focusing on e-mails and surfing the net for relevant information, later creating a web site.

5. Keeping abreast of change.
Legislation and taxation rules are constantly changing so that you need to ensure that your plan reflects current

practice and that you are aware of these changes and know how to react to them. The plan is not a static tool to be put on the shelf once it has been prepared; it is a dynamic tool to aid decision-making and to enable you to determine the impact of new situations as they arise.

PART II

Planning to plan

- Be clear about why you are preparing your business plan.
- Make sure you know what are the key elements of a business plan.
- Collect some basic information and set out your business idea in words.
- Be careful to take with you the people who will need to be satisfied with the plan.

6. The purpose of planning.

Business planning will help you (and others) to make better decisions **today,** taking all the relevant factors into account as far as you are able. It is not about making tomorrow's decisions. The plan is of critical importance to (a) the people who will put money into the business, as investors; (b) the people who lend money to the business, expecting to be paid back in due course and to receive interest on the loan; and (c) the people who will manage the business on a day-to-day basis. You may find that it is possible to obtain a grant to start-up or to improve your business: if so you will need to ensure that the needs of the grant-awarding body are also reflected in your plan.

In many small and medium-sized firms the most senior manager has a stake in the business as a partner or shareholder, and hence is an 'investor'. Other people, including managers or friends, may also put money into the venture, as investors, looking for a profit, but exposed to the possibility of a loss. Investors are interested in a 'return', in the profitability of the venture, in its survival and success. They will also need to pay attention to cash flow, because firms become bankrupt quickly if this is not controlled, even if they appear to be making a profit. Lenders will wish to be assured that they will be able to get their money back, and that interest payments can be sustained. This means that lenders are particularly interested in the cash flow forecasts, as these will indicate whether the money will be there to service loan repayments. The manager(s) will want to be confident that the methods to be used, the chosen location, the targets set, the costs involved and the prices to be charged for goods and services add up to a viable operation in practical terms in the market selected.

If a number of managers are involved, they may each have a particular interest in the plan according to the jobs which they hold. For example, a marketing and sales manager will pay close attention to such matters as the customer profiles, advertizing methods, sales techniques, pricing strategy, whilst the purchasing manager will look to the materials used, the anticipated costs and delivery times and the proposed level of bought-in materials to be held in stock.

Those who are responsible for making grants to organizations normally do this within the context of a policy – for example to promote employment in a deprived area, to stimulate the introduction of new technology, to enhance the skills of people in small firms or to improve the employment prospects of a disadvantaged group. If you seek such a grant you will need to ensure that the plan shows how the business activities will contribute to the grant-awarding body's policy.

You will be asked to work this out in more detail later, but throughout you must bear in mind the reason for planning – to enable you, your colleagues and your close business associates to make better decisions *NOW*.

7. Study the outline business plan.

See Figure 1. Look at each of the headings in turn. Your aim is to complete each section, and these are presented in the order in which they will appear in your completed plan. The means available for transmitting and receiving information are now many and varied. The use of the Internet has transformed the way most people conduct their businesses. You need to be sure that your take full account of these developments in your planning.

Figure 1.
OUTLINE BUSINESS PLAN
NAME OF THE BUSINESS ADDRESS OF THE BUSINESS NATURE OF THE BUSINESS PEOPLE IN THE BUSINESS, HEALTH AND SAFETY COMMUNICATIONS STRATEGY MARKETING AND SALES STRATEGY PROFIT AND LOSS FORECASTS CASH FLOW FORECASTS CAPITAL EXPENDITURE PLANS STOCK PURCHASING POLICY FUNDS REQUIRED – FINANCIAL BASE MANAGEMENT INFORMATION SPECIAL FACTORS including the ENVIRONMENT ACTION PLAN

It is important to recognize that you will not complete these sections in this order. Indeed, many of the items such as business name and address should not be completed until a number of decisions about the business have been made and recorded in other sections of the plan. A business – and hence a business plan – is not just a collection of bits and pieces. The varied aspects of the business – purchasing materials, reaching potential customers, providing goods and services, pricing these and generating cash and profit – are all interconnected.

This must be reflected in your plan. As each aspect is considered and new sums are done, other parts of the plan may need to be updated in the light of the results. This book takes you step by step through the planning process and lets you know when such updates and changes will be needed. In effect, every business decision you make, and every aspect of the business you describe is likely to have a bearing on the financial data. You will need constantly to come back to the profit and loss calculations and the cash flow forecasts, refining and improving them as each aspect of the business is dealt with in more detail, step by step.

8. Set out your planning timetable.
Study Figure 2. Make sure you cover all the angles and that all your preparation is completed on time. Bring this planning timetable out from time to time to check on your progress. Remember that as new information is assembled it will often be necessary to go back over your previous work and make adjustments.

For more help on each of the areas to be covered, refer to the section numbers in column two. Unless you have a great deal of experience and up-to-date knowledge of all the areas you need to cover, you will need to enlist the help of outside experts. Don't spend any

Figure 2. PLANNING TIMETABLE

ACTION	SECTIONS	PEOPLE AND METHODS	TARGET DATE	DATE ACHIEVED
PLANNING TO PLAN				
Plan to plan	6–9			
Collect information	10			
Make tentative decisions	11			
Sketch financial strategy	12			
Consider decision-makers	13–14			
ESSENTIAL EXPERTISE				
Enlist help	15–32			
Check your own skills	33–39			

KEY BUSINESS FACTORS									
Identify Key Factors	40–45								
Draft sections of plan	46–49								
Explore customers, competition, environment	50–55								
BASIC ESTIMATES									
Position products and services	56								
Estimate costs, prices and risks	57–60								
Consider location and premises	61								
Forecast sales and revenue	62–64								
Describe sales procedures	65–66								

11

ESSENTIAL CALCULATIONS									
Estimate capital requirements	67–68								
Estimate fixed and variable costs	69–77								
Review financial requirements	78–80								
Decide on stock levels	81								
Review finance and prepare balance sheets	82–85								
PLAN TO MANAGE									
Review key features of the plan	86–87								
Plan to manage business and people	88–91								
(Include critical path analysis)									

12

COLLATE YOUR PLAN						
Complete each section	92–104					
IMPLEMENTATION						
Finally review key checklists	105–109					
Deal with any deviations	111					
Update as required	112					

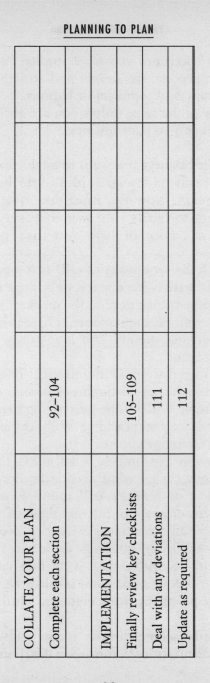

money on advice until you have studied Part II. Some parts of the process are simple and straightforward – others you may find technical or tedious. You must not miss out any of the steps unless you are absolutely sure they do not apply to your business.

9. Outline the business you want to establish or develop.
You may already have a good idea of the business you want to develop. Now you must take time to set this out on paper – to clarify your own thinking and to help others whose advice or help you may seek in due course.

What is it that you want to sell? Is it a product or a range of products? Is it a service, or a range of services? What will be your 'position' in the market? Will you be offering low volume, high quality at high prices, or high volume at modest quality and low prices? Or somewhere in between?

Do you intend to make the product or provide the services personally, or through employees, or through sub-contractors? Will you be purchasing raw materials, finished goods or components? Will you aim to franchise your idea in due course?

Who are your customers? What marks them out, or to put it another way, what need(s) do they have that your products or services will meet? How will you reach your customers – to interest them in your goods and services? On what basis will they decide to buy from you? Will your products or services be better, cheaper, more accessible than what they can get elsewhere? Or will your goods and services be unique – if so how have people or firms managed until now without them?

Will you be selling directly to the end-users (individuals or organizations?), through a distributor, directly (e.g. by mail order and deliveries), or through retail shops? What mark-up do you expect them to add to your prices? What methods of delivery will you adopt? Will you have your own delivery vehicles? If you provide a service, will you employ staff or sub-contract?

What after-sales and support services do you envisage? Will you provide this yourself or through a third party? Will you offer any guarantees over and above those required by law?

The most challenging question you must answer is this: 'Why should anyone buy my products and services, rather than those of my competitors?' If your only answer is that yours are cheaper, you should seriously consider giving up the idea now. Most sound businesses are based on more than just low prices. A business based purely on low prices is in constant danger of a powerful competitor undercutting that price – even at a loss – just to get the business.

What prices will you charge? Will you offer financial incentives to customers – discounts for prompt payment, rapid response or bulk orders? Pricing policies are discussed later. For now, recognize that in most cases you must charge what the market will bear, that is, what people are prepared to pay. This has got nothing whatever to do with what it costs you to provide, and everything to do with what benefit the purchaser believes he or she is getting. If you can provide your goods and services at a cost below the prices people will pay, you have a business. If you can't, don't start. Do some more sums! Restructure the business. The methods used to do these vital sums are described later on.

How do you expect to be paid? How soon will you need to set up the facility for your customers to pay by credit cards? If you intend to sell via the Internet, how will you collect payment?

10. Start to collect the basic information you will need.
Now that you have a good grasp of the business you want to develop, you can start to gather information about your potential customers, competitors and the business environment. When you have identified your potential customers, find out how many there are, how often they will buy the kinds of goods and services you intend to offer, what they look for, and what they are prepared to spend. Are you offering goods that are purchased once a week, once a year or only on special occasions? Where do they shop? Where else do these people go, what newspapers and magazines do they read? Do they use the Internet? What arrangements will you make with search engines and what will this cost? You must decide what factors matter to you, and start to gather information on these. Remember that you want to keep on selling – so you need an adequate supply of potential customers. Now start to think about those providers who will be in competition with you. First of all, consider any other business offering similar products or services. Are they aiming at the same market – to sell to the same people as yourself? If so, what do you consider to be their strengths and weaknesses – in terms of product quality, price, delivery, convenience, packaging, presentation and so forth. Then again consider people who offer an alternative to your products or services. Consider how your products are used. Consider how you are going to make your products and services more attractive to the customers. In effect whenever you offer a product there is also a service – for example in terms of ease of ordering, delivery times, returns policy and ease of payment.

Don't fall into the trap of making your products 'better' in a way that appeals to you, but may not appeal to your customers. If you make it 'better' than your competitors maybe you will have to charge a higher price. That is OK if the customers are happy to pay the price for the improvement – but if not, you are in trouble.

Consider the business environment. Are there any developments which will impact on your plans – e.g. new regulations with which you will need to comply, changes in the price of raw materials, changing patterns of spending, new techniques for manufacture or service provision. We shall discuss all these matters in a little more detail later, but for now, make a list of the items you consider important in relation to your own business, and revise your plans accordingly.

11. Make some tentative decisions.
Now is the time to set out the conclusions you have reached so far about your business idea. See how much of Figure 3 you can complete.

These initial decisions may well need to be revised as your work proceeds.

12. Sketch out your financial strategy.
How much money will you need to get going? What will you need to spend on property, equipment, furniture, telephone installations, initial advertizing (including any required for recruitment purposes), licences, stocks (e.g. raw materials, finished goods for sale, stationary) and Internet services? Make a rough estimate – to the nearest £1 or £10. Where will this money come from?

From the above, work out when the money will come in from sales, then estimate when fresh bills will fall due – for wages, gas, electricity, rent and so on. Will you need 'working capital' to keep the business going? Where will this come from? If you need to borrow any money to cover the initial expenditure or the cash flow

Figure 3. Outline Business Idea

	Estimate how much you will sell in one year in each case.	Taking into account late payments and bad debts, how much income do you expect in the year in each case?
Where will your business operate from?		
Who will be your customers?		
How will you reach these customers and interest them in your wares?		
List below your products and services, the quality levels, and prices to be charged:		
1.		
2.		
3.		
4.		
5.		
TOTAL		

18

requirements, what will you offer as security, and how much will the interest and capital repayments cost? As your ideas are firmed up, you will need to work this out in detail, but you may find it useful to do some rough and ready sums now.

You should be careful not to borrow too much money relative to your own investment. See the discussion on gearing in Section 78.

13. Identify the key decision makers.
Remember that in drawing up your plans you need to consider all the people who will have a financial stake in the business, and who may wish to study your business plan, i.e.

- **investors** – those who put money in hoping for a profit at the end of the day (and are prepared to risk taking a loss), and this probably includes you;
- **lenders** – those who lend you their money and expect to get it back, with interest paid regularly and on time along the way, and repayments as agreed, possibly in phases;
- **officials** – in grant-awarding bodies, who will wish to ensure that your finances are sound and that your plans show how your business will fulfil the grant aims and conditions.

Governments (for example at National and European level) and a number of charitable trusts are prepared to give grants to commercial organizations provided they meet strict conditions. The officials who work for such bodies are likely to have two key concerns: the objectives of the grant and how they will be met and the viability of the commercial organization. Usually when a public body offers a grant, the scheme forms a part of an overall strategy to bring about a change of some sort, for example, to improve the prosperity of a geographical area, to encourage a particular type of trade, to generate employment, or to accelerate the introduction of new technology.

Thus when you prepare your business plan and engage in discussions with such officials, you must demonstrate how your activities will promote the aims of the public body. These considerations go beyond the normal requirements of a business plan, but they are essential if you seek a grant. By studying the aims and objectives of the public body and the criteria for the award you can draw up a plan that meets both business objectives and also the needs of the grant-awarding body. If the grant is for employment generation, for example, estimate the number of jobs the business will generate and when.

Public officials tend to judge viability on the quality of the people who will manage the operation as well as the validity of the written plan. Include a detailed curriculum vitae for each of the key managers who will be involved in running the business, showing the expertise and experience that they will bring to the operation. Demonstrate how these managers have been forged into a team who are dedicated to the organization's goals.

The senior people who are expected to **manage** the business should be involved in the planning process and convinced of the viability of the final business plan. If your organization is big enough to have managers responsible for different parts of the plan – such as marketing and sales, production, distribution, credit control – each must be convinced that their part is sound.

Although they may not see your planning documents, there are other groups who need to be taken into account in planning, e.g.

20

- **suppliers** who give you goods on credit terms, expecting a reliable customer who will pay bills on time, and keep in business giving repeat orders;
- **regular customers** who expect consistent products, and associated services (e.g. delivery and invoicing procedures);
- **employees** who hope for adequate remuneration and employment conditions, job security and continuity of employment.

You should also take into account the public authorities relevant to your business – the bodies responsible for tax and National Insurance, Value added tax, the environment (including disposal of waste etc.), health and safety matters, any regulations specific to your business, e.g. relating to premises, dangerous equipment or to trade activities. There may be bodies that are crucial in your industry and where membership is virtually a requirement to conduct your business – for example in some building trades, financial operations or travel.

In recent years, particularly in Europe and the USA, there has been an avalanche of new regulations related to health and safety, the environment and employment issues (for example on part-time workers, temporary workers, sub-contractors, diversity, maternity and paternity leave) and social security. You will need to consider how you will keep abreast of such developments and how they will impact on your business. This may involve, for example, expenditure on key publications or subscriptions to relevant small business or trade associations: these costs will be included in your 'publications and subscriptions' heading later.

14. List the requirements of the key decision makers.

Identify, by name or job title (e.g. bank manager, co-investor) each person involved in making decisions about your business based on the plan, and put these names on the left hand side of Figure 4. Now summarize briefly, on the right hand side, what you consider to be the deciding factor in their decision – e.g. an ability to pay 4 per cent over base rate, or a prospect of a 20 per cent return on investment, or an adequate advertizing budget.

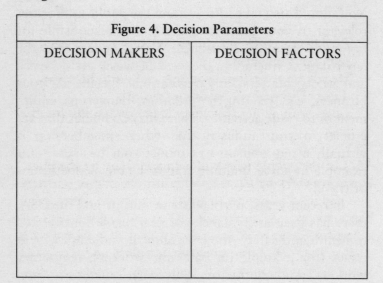

Figure 4. Decision Parameters	
DECISION MAKERS	DECISION FACTORS

PART III

Essential expertise

- Review carefully all the expertise you will need to plan your business.
- Decide on the people you will call on to help you.
- Take charge of the 'planning group'.
- Check out your own knowledge and skills for the task.

15. List the people who will help you draw up the plan.
If you are working alone or with just one or two partners you will need to review the gaps in your own knowledge and expertise. If there are one or more partners, co-directors, or senior managers who will be working with you on the plan, write down their names and alongside make a note of the skills they bring to the job (e.g. knowledge of marketing, management accounts, retailing etc.). You may require more skills from time to time – e.g. in tax planning, property matters, and for this you may need to engage the services of specialists.

You may also need to give some thought to people who may not be involved closely in the planning, but whose expertise will be needed in the business and who might make a useful comment on your ideas. In your business you may need people with specific qualifica-

Figure 5. People Involved in Planning

FACTOR	NAME OF PERSON CONCERNED	OTHERS INVOLVED OR CONSULTED	DATE CONSULTATION PLANNED	DATE CONSULTATION COMPLETED
Sales forecasting				
Production				
Sales promotion				
Purchasing policy				
Delivery systems				
Sales and invoicing				
Computers and the Internet				
Pricing policy				
Tax planning				
Employing people				
Environment				
Health and safety				
Contracts				

tions – e.g. to drive particular vehicles, to manage a distribution operation, to manage a travel agency.

Consider the factors identified in Figure 5. Draw up your own list, using this one as a starting point. As your planning progresses, pull this list out from time to time, adding more headings if they become necessary. Cross out any headings in the list if they do not apply to your business. The first column lists key issues which can make or break your business, and the second the people who will help you to work on these aspects of the plan. Use the third column to indicate whether they are to be included in the planning team (put 'T'), or be consulted (write 'C'). The last two columns are to help you put a target date to consult key people and to indicate this has been achieved.

16. Check the expertise you need.
Next, look through the checklist of expertise provided in the following paragraphs and in Figure 6 make a note, in the right hand column, of how you intend to provide this.

17. Secure accountancy advice, especially on taxation matters.
You will need advice on how to record and to present financial information and how to make proper provision for national insurance and taxes (e.g. income tax, corporation tax and value added tax). You may also need advice on using a computer and the Internet for financial information and for trading purposes. You need to make a careful note of any returns that you are required to submit and the key dates involved.

18. Secure marketing advice or services.
It is important for you to identify and investigate your potential customers thoroughly. If your business is

Figure 6. Expertise Requirements	
Expertise	Provision
Accountancy	
Marketing	
Advertizing	
Sales	
Export/Import	
Form of Business	
Insurance – General	
Insurance – Life and Key Person	
Interpretation/Translation	
Legal	
Patents, Copyrights, Trade Marks	
Property and Location	
Employment	
Health and Safety	
Environmental Protection	
Food Hygiene	
Technical Writing	
Trade Matters	
People Relationships	

straightforward this will not be a complicated matter. You may be able to get the information you require by talking to a number of potential customers personally. In many cases, however, you may be unaware of the many ways available for gathering information about potential customers – and competitors. Be careful to keep expenditure within realistic constraints. Advice should not be too expensive, but market surveys are generally costly.

19. Secure sales advice.
You may well consider this is not necessary, but there is a lot to learn about stimulating interest in your products

and services, presenting appropriate benefits and persuading people to make that 'purchasing decision'. Your success depends on these 'purchasing decisions' and you must ensure that you have the expertise to bring this off. It has been said that a sale is not a sale until the payment reaches your bank account. Ensure that you know how to monitor sales receipts and what action to take when people do not pay, or are constantly late in paying.

20. Secure advertizing advice or services.

Poor advertizing is a waste of money: in many cases this is a specialist area where a little advice from experts is well worthwhile. To be successful, advertizing must reach an adequate number of potential clients, it must arouse their interest, evoke a reaction and lead to a purchasing decision. If you are in any doubt about how to reach that result, seek help. The percentage response to advertizing can be very disappointing. There are also some inexpensive ways to promote your business, e.g. issuing press releases as opportunities arise.

If you use the Internet for advertizing or selling your products and services you will need to consider how to get people to log on to your web site. You may need to advertise this in other media (e.g. magazines) and also consider how to ensure that potential customers who use the major search engines are directed to your site.

21. Secure exporting or importing advice and services.

If you intend to import goods or to export goods or services it is important that you understand both the formal procedures and practices involved – but equally that you understand something of the custom and practices of the business people in the countries with whom you intend to trade.

22. Secure advice on form of business.

You must decide very early whether you intend to conduct your business as a sole trader, or in partnership with others, or as a limited company. You may also need to consider whether to take up or to offer a franchise. There are tax and legal implications in each case, and you need to talk these through with an expert (e.g. your accountant or a solicitor). In particularly complex cases you my need the help of a solicitor who specializes in such matters.

23. Secure insurance advice and services.

There are a number of insurable risks to be taken into account, according to the nature of your business. Think through what you need and then seek the advice of a qualified insurance broker for all your general requirements. You should also consider personal, partnership and key person insurance, and pension planning and here you need to consult a qualified life insurance specialist.

24. Consider interpretation and translation services.

When you need language services for interpretation or translation it is often urgent, so it may be useful to make enquiries about available services at an early stage. In general, try to get people who will interpret or translate into their own native tongue for the best results, e.g. where you are conducting a business meeting or preparing a letter or printed matter for an overseas client.

25. Secure legal advice and services.

You should seek legal advice on partnership agreements and commercial contracts, including those for equipment or vehicle leasing or hire, as well as those concerned with sales and straightforward purchasing. As mentioned previously, you will also need legal advice if you enter into franchizing.

26. Consider advice and services on patents, copyright, trade and service marks.

This whole area is complex and regulated, so that if you consider that you are likely to be involved in any way, you should seek proper advice from qualified experts.

27. Secure advice and/or services on property matters and location.

You will need to consider carefully what property you will need, whether to buy, rent or lease. Here you should seek the advice of a qualified surveyor who is well acquainted with the area in which you wish to locate your business. The importance of locating your operation in the optimum position and in appropriate accommodation cannot be over stressed. You will also need to consider carefully how you will use the premises, who will visit and deliver (in what type of vehicles), and what services (gas, water, electricity, drainage etc.) you will require. Do not forget to take into consideration the needs of disabled people who will need to gain access to your premises and need safe means of escape in an emergency.

28. Secure advice and/or services on employment matters.

The public employment services will give you a lot of help and guidance. You will need to consider carefully how best to recruit and select people, and the various rules concerning employment, including National Insurance payments and taxation of employees. Remember there are now strict rules about hours of work, discrimination, dismissal procedures, employment contracts and so forth.

Legislation in this area has changed markedly in recent years and is likely to continue to change, so it is essential that you keep up-to-date and have quick access to a source of help and advice when a problem arises.

You must also consider how to help your employees to gain the skills they need to make your business a success. You may be able to recruit people who have many of the skills required, but business does not stand still. New developments change the way that tasks are done, especially in the field of communications. Your competitors will employ modern methods, even if you do not, giving them the edge. Public bodies now offer help and advice on training and many courses are now available through the Internet. See also Sections 39 and 49.

Managing diversity within the people you employ or who could apply for employment involves seeking out and removing the obstacles that individuals face as they seek for advancement – whether this is related to gender, race, creed, background, personality, sexual orientation, life-style, age or disability. A progressive policy also looks at other issues, such as employees responsible for caring for children or for sick or elderly relatives. It will also ensure that people are not disadvantaged because of their accent or where they live.

29. Secure information on health and safety.

Whether you employ other people or not, your business activities will be covered by the various regulations relating to health and safety – in the workplace, in the goods and services you supply, and in relation to the general public and the environment. If you have anything to do with food – even providing sandwiches to your staff – you must consider the impact of Food Hygiene regulations.

Legislation in the field of health and safety has to be

considered in relation to your operation. What procedures and provisions (e.g. first aid equipment, trained first aid people and escape routes) will you need to put in place?

30. Secure information on environmental matters.
There can be very few businesses, if any, that have no effect on the environment – not least in the disposal of 'waste'. Legislation in this field is developing rapidly, usually incurring business costs and restrictions on the way you conduct your operation. Your trade or professional body may be the best starting point for information on these issues.

31. Consider technical writing services.
You may have technical expertise or technical experts on your staff that really know their stuff – but can they express technical ideas in simple language? Here the help of a technical author can be valuable, e.g. in the preparation of technical sales literature or manuals for customers.

32. Secure advice on trade matters.
Even if you are on top of your trade it is still worth making contact with any trade or professional bodies operating in your field. They should be able to keep you up-to-date with current trends in the marketplace, prices of raw materials, new methods and materials being developed, new legislation being considered and so on. If there is no specific body for your trade, consider subscribing to an organization that supports small firms.

33. Lead the planning group.
If you are the person in charge of planning a new business or developing a new plan for an existing business,

you need to gather around you a small team involving those who will help you manage the business – your partners, co-directors and managers. It is clear from the preceding paragraphs that your team will need to draw on a variety of expertise and information if the plan is to be soundly based.

In this context, leadership means making sure that each member of the team shares the vision of the business, and really wants it to succeed. You must be prepared to talk this through honestly, and listen to any problems people have and face up to them. At this stage there is nothing to be gained by sweeping problems under the carpet. They must be surfaced and resolved. Make sure each member of the team has a clear idea of what is expected and when. Refer back to Figure 2, which you may use as a template for planning and involving people.

If you are writing this plan on your own, you will certainly need people to talk to about it from time to time. A number of sources of advice, consultancy and training are available, and you need to seek out someone you can trust and who will give you honest feedback and advice.

34. Business leadership.

The man or woman at the top must have the breadth of vision to see the business as a whole and to know how the various parts fit together. There is no better way to get to know these interconnections than preparing a business plan from scratch. You are advised to take stock of your personal 'skill mix' and to take steps to make up any shortfall at the earliest opportunity.

In the following paragraphs we will consider briefly five key knowledge/skill areas for the person at the top:

- the trade itself
- business parameters
- marketing and sales methods
- money management
- managing people relationships

35. Master the trade know-how.

You must achieve a reasonable level of knowledge, and some skills, in the type of business you are embarking upon, the tools of the trade, the methods used, the skills involved and the key factors for success. You may also need to know something about the culture in that trade – 'the way we do things around here'. Remember that a sound business is often built on relationships with people, and ignorance of the trade is no recommendation.

36. Grasp the business parameters.

You need to be on top of the parameters used in your kinds of business, typical quantities (size of warehouse, capacity of vehicles, turnover, cost factors, profit margins, contractual arrangements and credit terms. You are not bound to follow the normal practices in the trade, but you should have a very sound reason for going your own way. The unusual way you propose to do business may be your 'Unique Selling Point', what marks out your market niche – but it could easily be your downfall. Be sure you know what you are doing before you try to buck the system. It may, at first sight, seem easy for you to get a better return on your investment than anybody else – but it is more likely that you have overlooked some crucial factor.

37. Delve into marketing.

If you are not an expert you will need advice. But do not leave everything to the experts. You must gain a basic understanding of certain principles and how they apply to your business. You need to know how to research your products and services, how to study the market, how to get information about your customers, what questions to ask, how to estimate demand, to determine the optimum price/quality/service level provisions, how to identify your market segment. Others can do the detailed work – but you must know enough to remain in charge.

You need to be able to discuss with confidence the selection of advertizing media and methods, about advertizing copy, technical brochures, selling methods, negotiating techniques, sales force management and merchandizing.

38. Controlling the money.

You must become adept at estimating costs, forecasting and managing cash flow, calculating profit and loss, reading balance sheets, assessing alternative financial strategies, making decisions about the source and application of funds. It is not so much the arithmetic – it is understanding what the figures mean for the business and what actions to take when the figures seem to go wrong. You will have to get to know some of the technical terms like depreciation, liquidity and gearing. Remember that every figure in your plan has a basis, and it is more important to know what that is than to remember a particular number. You must manage cash flow from day one, and you will need to show a profit before too long to stay in business. **The skill of managing money is a top priority.**

In many businesses there is an initial start-up period when the expenditure vastly exceeds income. You must plan for this and ensure that your financial arrangements are robust enough to survive this period. Often it takes time to compile a list of potential customers, to build customer confidence and to secure orders. It will take longer to secure income from sales: remember that a sale cannot be regarded as secure until the cash is in your business bank account. In the early stages your suppliers may be unwilling to give you much credit.

You must make a rigid distinction between your business finance and your personal accounts, even if you are a sole trader. This is not simply to enable you to comply with the tax authorities, but it is to ensure that you have a firm and unequivocal grasp of your business.

39. Managing people relationships.
In virtually every business the man or woman at the top has to be able to deal effectively with people – including the bank manager, the tax inspector, the customers, the suppliers, advisors and (above all!) colleagues – co-directors, partners, managers and other employees. In every case, skills are involved and building constructive relationships usually makes a very real difference to the success of the business.

In the case of employees the law is now complex and full of pitfalls for the unwary. This legalistic side can be dealt with, but now employers are recognizing the need to win the full support of every employee, to help them gain the expertise they need and to weld them into an effective team, so that the customer feels welcome and cared for and the quality of goods and services is maintained at a high level at all times. This calls for sensitive leadership.

Doing business with people of different races and background, and with people who speak a different language, is full of pitfalls and calls for patience and perhaps some background study and advice.

PART IV

Key business factors

- Compile a checklist of the key factors for success in your business.
- Describe your business on paper in some detail.
- Take an in-depth look at your potential customers.
- Check out your competitors and their wares.
- Review the environment for your business.

40. Review how your colleagues and advisors are involved in planning.
Refer to Figure 2. If other people are helping you with parts of the planning process, and perhaps with some of the drafting of text, now is the moment to review the situation and to ensure that everyone knows what is expected of them, and by what date.

41. Make up your own checklist of key factors.
The feasibility of your business plan depends on proper management, sound marketing and secure financial management. Review the checklists provided in the following paragraphs. (These checklists are reproduced from *The 24-Hour Business Plan*.) Draw up your own list based on these ideas – deleting any that seem inappropriate, and adding any further factors you consider

crucial. As the plan builds up, see how many of these questions you can tick off as answered.

42. Management checklist.

- Do you and your management team have the motivation and the technical skills to make the products or services you envisage?
- Do you and your management team have all the skills needed to look after the administrative side of the business, including money matters?
- Has your organization the ability to sell your goods/services to the potential customers you have identified?
- Are you prepared to modify your business plans in the light of what people will want to buy?
- Are you confident that you and your key managers will be able to manage skills and time to full effect?
- Do you have access to the information technology skills you need?
- Have you and your management team developed the approach needed to deal with the officials of public funding bodies – if that is required?
- Does your management team have the ability to cope with the multitude of demands for compliance with the law, for example in terms of taxation, employment, contracts and environmental issues?

43. Marketing checklist.

- What is so special about the product that you intend to sell or the service that you intend to provide?
- How do you know that anyone will want to buy them?
- How much will you charge for your products/services? Will people be prepared to pay those prices?
- Are you sure that you can provide those goods/services at these prices, make a profit and manage cash flow?

- Why should anyone buy your goods/services rather than others on the market?
- Is this the right time to start providing the goods/services that you have in mind? Is this the moment when people will want them?
- Will you be able to develop your product or develop new products as your market develops?
- Have you considered how you will advertise or promote your product and how much this will cost?
- Do you know who your competitors are and what products they are selling?
- Have you spoken to any potential customers about the product/service that you intend to provide?

44. Money management checklist.
- Will your business make a profit?
- Will you be able to pay each bill when it arrives?
- What financial resources will you need to be successful, especially over the initial trading period?
- Are you fully prepared to make your share of this financial commitment?
- Do you need – can you obtain – a loan at a reasonable rate of interest?
- Are you confident that you can pay back any loans over a reasonable period, and pay the interest?
- Have you researched, listed and determined the expenditures that you will incur, and when income will start to flow?
- Have you considered your insurance needs and any licences and permits that will be required?
- What sources of information, help and advice do you need? Do you know where these can be obtained?
- Have you discovered any problems that you have never had to deal with before?

45. Plan to deal with any special factors in your business.
Consider carefully whether you will need any special licences or permits to operate your business, or to use the premises, vehicles or equipment for particular purposes, or to store particular materials. Are there any special risks, or particular kinds of insurance you will need to make provision for? Remember that in some instances insurance is legally required, e.g. if you have employees. These things may take a lot of time to arrange, and will need to be brought into the plan.

46. Prepare drafts of key sections of the plan.
Where you have information to hand, start to draft out the text of key sections of the plan, so that it starts to build up. Review Figure 1 to see which sections you feel you can now tackle.

Draft a preliminary 'Nature of the Business' statement. Write down in simple terms the essential features of your business – what goods and services you will offer, to whom and to what standards, highlighting what is special about your approach. Refer to Figure 3, Section 6 for further help. This statement will help you and your colleagues to focus on the key elements in the business.

47. Do a Quick Check over your business idea.
Using your draft 'Nature of the Business', any sections you have drafted and the data you have gathered so far, review your earlier answers to the Management, Marketing and Money checklists above. Can you improve on your previous replies?

48. Set out a more detailed description of your business.
Refer to your answers to the 'quick-check' questions. You must now provide a much more detailed statement of the nature of your business, describing your cus-

tomers, the precise products and services you will offer, how you will reach your customers, and how you will sell, how you will obtain any materials you will need, and provide your products and services. All these factors will need to be more closely defined as described in the following sections.

49. Plan to develop skills and knowledge.

Check that you have the skills and knowledge you will need to make a success of your business. Be sure you have these in support of your business at the appropriate level. This breakdown of skills will be based on the way you now see your business developing. You may have all the skills you need personally – but this is unlikely. Where will the extra skills you need come from? Will you rely on your external advisors? Do you have colleagues in the business (e.g. partners, fellow directors, senior managers) who have the skills required? In some businesses people will need to have qualifications to carry out certain functions e.g. driving fork lift trucks, taking charge of a transport operation, running a racecourse, an airfield, an employment agency or providing investment advice.

Summarize your decisions in a 'people' statement, amplifying at this stage what training or development plans you have for yourself, your senior colleagues and your employees. Refer back to Figure 6, Section 16, 'Expertise Requirements' for your checklist.

50. Focus on your customers.

Investigate your potential customers carefully. Study them with every tool at your disposal. You need to know all about your customers so that your advertizing and sales activity will hit the target. Identify your 'market segment' and hence your 'niche' in the market.

You will need to gather information on your market sector so that you may focus more closely on your preferred customers. Remember that the decision to buy – or not to buy – is made by one or more people in each case, not by inanimate companies or corporations. Ask yourself constantly, 'why should these people decide to buy from me?'

If your potential customers are individual members of the public you will need to consider what is special about them, where they live, what are their interests, what magazines they read, what entertainment they seek, and how much disposable income they have to spend on your type of products and services. How do they buy such things – from shops, through the Internet or by mail order? Are such purchases carefully weighed decisions, or simply on impulse? Do people buy such things rarely – or often? How often – every day, every week, every month? Or only for Christmas?

If you sell to the public through retail outlets, these outlets together with your customers and their needs, (e.g. for merchandizing support or a clear returns policy,) must be taken into account.

If your potential customers are corporate bodies – firms, government departments or local authorities, what are their current sources of supply? What do their current suppliers provide – by way of products, services, after-sales service, frequency of delivery, financial arrangements? What are their purchasing arrangements? Do they each have a purchasing department? Who makes the decision to purchase your kinds of products and services? There may be more than one person involved. Who influences the people who decide? What criteria are used to decide which supplier to use? Are there conditions – e.g. do they require adherence to specific standards – technical or quality assurance? Does your product require after-sales support? If so how will this be provided?

Above all, how will you gain the confidence of the decision makers?

51. Segment your market.

There are several steps to work through in considering your market. Typically the steps involve:

- listing the geographical areas in which you will seek to trade with your customers, i.e. to cover your town or county, your country or continent, or the whole world, and noting how many prospective customers there are in that area;
- listing the characteristics and desires of the people likely to buy from you (if you sell to the public), or the particular concerns of those who make or influence purchasing decisions in organizations;
- listing the likely requirements and concerns of any intermediaries you might be dealing with (e.g. distributors, agents, wholesalers), and the characteristics of those most likely to deal in your particular goods and services;
- listing the characteristics of the kinds of organizations you want to do business with – their number, size, key decision makers, purchasing policies, payment performance and so forth.

Remember that if you deal through intermediaries you have to satisfy their legitimate business needs as well as the requirements of your end purchaser. In dealing with organizations you will need to think through the people who will influence buying decisions, what their concerns are, and how to both reach them and convince them that your products and services will really meet their particular needs. This often means that your people will need to approach more than one person in a given organization, and that the different people involved will have different concerns, e.g. the purchasing offer with quality and value for money, but the technical manager with the ability to perform precisely what he or she wants. You will need to take account of such factors in your marketing and sales strategy.

52. Focus on your market niche.
It is tempting to produce a wide range of goods and services for a wide range of customers. That generally leads to chaos and failure. Every extra type of product and every different type of customer stretches your resources further – in terms of management time and effort, in terms of the multiplicity of different products you need to keep and the number of contacts you need to maintain and media you need to use for advertizing. You really must focus down on either a narrow range of products or a narrow range of customers. Identifying this 'niche' in the market and why you have a special advantage in that niche is the key to a successful business idea. Consider what 'image' you wish to project to your customers and how you will achieve this.

53. Consider your competitors.
What do you actually know about your existing and potential competitors? What goods and services are they offering to your potential clients? What are the special features of their products and services which attract custom? Are they developing new ideas which you need to know about? What is their 'position' in the marketplace, compared to your own? (See Section 55.)

54. Define your products and services.

Design your products and services in the light of this information about your potential customers and what you have found out about the competitors and how customers view their wares. It is by studying these factors that you will be helped to identify how you can be different, but in a way that pleases your customers and attracts good business. Be careful not to overload your products and services with features that customers neither want, nor need, nor will benefit from. All this will increase the price, but not the desirability of the product. At the end of the day good business comes from giving people benefits that they feel good about.

It may be that you have a product or service never before offered to these customers. You need to make a judgement about the acceptability of your offerings. Talk to experts who will give you advice. In most cases carefully controlled trials will be needed before embarking on large-scale investment.

55. Review your environmental scan.

Review the business climate for your business and any significant external factors. Take into account any political and legislative matters that could effect your business – e.g. business rates, interest rates, exchange rates, new license requirements, new standards for products or services. Are there any economic, social or technological factors to take into account?

It is worthwhile taking time out to examine these four factors at a level of detail suitable to your business. In the following paragraphs there are some leading questions to help you with this analysis. In each case, consider whether these matters are relevant, and if so what effect they will have on your business and how you will take this into account (see Figure 7).

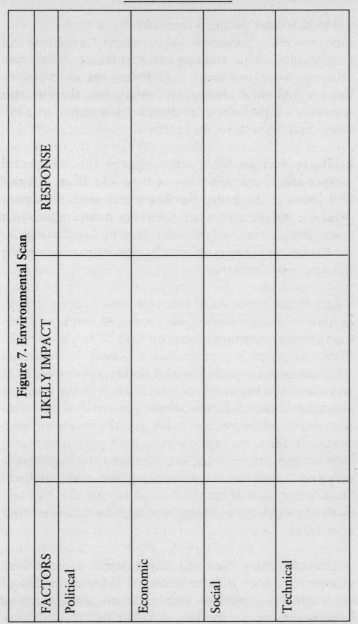

Figure 7. Environmental Scan

FACTORS	LIKELY IMPACT	RESPONSE
Political		
Economic		
Social		
Technical		

Political factors: What is the current government's attitude towards business? What about the European Community? What changes can you foresee which will influence your business? Will there, for example, be more legislation on health and safety, on race discrimination, on equal opportunities, on consumer or environmental protection, on taxation?

Economic factors: What price changes can be expected – especially in relation to your supplies? What is likely to happen to exchange rates, interest rates, inflation? Who has the discretionary spending power now? Is it young people – or well off older people? Are the requirements for your kinds of goods and services generally growing – or declining?

Social factors: You must consider these factors in connection with their impact on your customers, but they may also be important when you wish to employ people. What are people's expectations nowadays – concerned with involvement in decisions, equality, quality of life at work and the work–life balance? What is the effect of changing household expenditure patterns? What effect does the structure of households (e.g. the balance of one-parent families, or partners who both go out to work) have on your trade? What are the expectations of people concerned with the environment, noise and nuisance? Such factors can affect the cost of labour, the expectations of employees and suppliers, and the desires of your customers.

Technical factors: How will developments in technology change the nature of your business? What is the impact of improved communication systems and changing banking practices? The use of technology in communications and funds transfer coupled with any changes in technology in your particular trade must be taken fully into account in your planning. Are there specific technological developments that might alter the nature of your products or services?

PART V

Basic estimates

- Decide on a 'position' in the market for your goods and services.
- Consider the prices you will charge and estimate costs and likely profit.
- Think about where your business will be located and your business address.
- How will you advertise, sell and be paid for your goods and services?
- Estimate what you can sell and set sales targets.

56. Position your products and services.
We are all familiar with the fact that many products and services can be offered at different levels – a handkerchief or a ball point pen can be simply made from inexpensive materials and sold in quantity at a low price, or exquisitely decorated and carefully crafted to produce a prestige item commanding a high price. You must decide where to place your products and services in this sense – what we call 'positioning' (see Figure 8).

57. Revise pricing structure.
You must fix on some price levels now so that you can do further calculations, but these prices may need to be

Figure 8. Positioning

	LOW PRICE	MEDIUM PRICE	HIGH PRICE
HIGH QUALITY			High-quality speciality goods and services can command high prices and profit margins, but expect modest sales.
MODERATE QUALITY		Products and services of modest but sound quality in the middle price range can generate healthy profits.	
LOW QUALITY	Inexpensive products and services have a place in the marketplace: profit margins may be low, and this means that high volumes are essential for a profitable business.		

49

reviewed again once you have done your sums. The relationship between the prices you charge to customers and the costs incurred in providing goods and services may seem straightforward, but in practice it is not. This is because the cost per item actually depends on the quantities you sell. If you make a product, the cost per item is dependent on how many you can sell, not just on the quantities you produce.

If you are in the business of tendering for contracts then you must base your price estimates on a cost-plus basis – being careful to investigate and take full account of the precise requirements of the customer, especially in terms of the quality required and the likely sum he or she will pay. In other words you will need to determine what the customer wants, decide how to provide this, work out what it will cost you, and then add a profit margin. You then have to consider the quality verses cost and how your customer will react.

In most businesses, the cost plus idea, i.e. working out what it costs to produce an item or provide a service, and using this cost plus a profit margin to fix the price you charge has a number of drawbacks. In most businesses this method is inappropriate and should not be used. In manufacture, for example, there is the problem of allocating overheads. This becomes even more problematic when the same machines and people make a range of products. In this procedure the allocation of overheads depends on the sales prediction. An alternative approach is to separate out the overhead costs and then to calculate the gross profit on each product – and to view this as a contribution to overhead costs / profit.

The profitability of the business is then calculated as the sum of the gross profit from each 'line' (i.e. each type of product or service) less the fixed costs. A simple sum will show that as long as you can keep your overheads the same, the costs per item reduces as the number of items you can make *and sell* increases. The same basic argument applies to services, where employees must be paid irrespective of the income derived from the services they provide. Clearly there comes a point where the overheads must increase when sales increase, and a new overhead figure must be applied. Paying bonuses to staff on the basis of their sales complicates the arithmetic. Be careful to ensure that bonuses work for the company as well as for the employees concerned.

The most important problem with the cost-plus method is that people pay according to the benefit they consider they receive, rather than according to the work involved, and they will compare price and quality, and arrive at what they consider to be value for money. In other words, your price should be determined by what the market will bear – not on your costs. This emphasizes the need for thorough market research. As remarked earlier, you must make your goods and provide your services below this price to make a profit. It is on this basis that you should list all your products and services and the prices you will charge in each case.

There may be occasions when you can charge much more than your costs – but this situation is not likely to last: sell at this price while you can, because later you may have to sell the same product at a price that will barely recover costs. However, if you want to stay in business you should avoid any action which smacks of cheating the customer or offering a poor deal. You may wish to offer a product or service at below cost – e.g. as a loss leader to bring in other business, or as an initial attraction to get customers to try your goods and services. Make sure you have recorded your intentions and that you include an explanation of your basic pricing philosophy and methods in your business plan.

58. Prepare basic estimates on costs, price and profit.

A more detailed explanation of the factors involved is presented in Part VI; at this stage use rough estimates of the key factors to check out your ideas. From the pricing structure you have provisionally determined and your estimate of sales, forecast the profit you expect from the business over the first year of operation.

See Figure 9. First list out your products and services and for each one estimate the income to be generated in the year (volume of sales × price). Then subtract the variable costs incurred – i.e. any costs incurred which are specific to the product or service (e.g. if you are a retailer the cost you paid to purchase the items you have sold), to give the gross profit for each product/service line. Add up the gross profit from each line and then deduct the overheads to give the net profit to the business.

When you come to do these calculations in more detail there are other factors to take into account, e.g. income from other sources – such as interest on bank deposits, and asset sales.

59. Estimate the business risks involved.

Armed with this data you can now do some sums to indicate the level of risk involved – e.g. if your sales fall below expectations, or if key raw materials rise in price. A simple way to do this is illustrated in Figure 10. In row 1 calculate the income you expect to generate from sales if they are, in the event, 'poor' i.e. the worst sales you can anticipate, then what you can reasonably expect, then higher than expected, and finally very high sales figures. In row 2, estimate the variable costs, i.e. the cost to your business of the items sold in each case. In row 3 you can estimate the gross profit and by deducting the fixed costs (row 4) you can estimate profit levels for various sales levels, including the financial risks of low

Figure 9. Rough Estimate of Anticipated Profit

List of products and/or services	Sales anticipated in the first year	Income to be generated, i.e. estimate of number of items sold × price	Variable costs incurred, i.e. number of items sold × variable cost/item	Gross profit for each line in the first year
A				
B				
C				
D				
E				
			TOTAL GROSS PROFIT	
			Less Overheads	
			Total Profit/Loss	

N.B. A sales level may be reached where the overheads must be increased.

Figure 10. Estimation of Risk

	POOR SALES	EXPECTED SALES	HIGH SALES	VERY HIGH SALES
1. Price charged × quantity sold				
2. Cost / item × number sold (variable costs)				
3. Gross Profit = (unit price – unit costs) × sales volume				
4. Fixed Costs				
5. Net Profit (Gross Profit less Fixed Costs)				

Figure 10a. Example of Risk Analysis				
Items sold	20	50	70	150
Price (£10) x Sales	£200	£500	£700	£1,500
Variable Cost (£4/item)	£80	£200	£280	£600
Gross Profit	£120	£300	£420	£900
Fixed Costs	£300	£300	£300	£300
Profit/(Loss)	(£180)	**Breakeven**	£120	£600

sales. This procedure is often called 'sensitivity analysis' – see Figure 10a.

You can use the same approach to estimate other factors, e.g. increased unit costs or fixed costs. (You can also use this approach to forecast instances where, having committed outlay on overheads it may be preferable to proceed even when a loss is incurred, because the loss would be greater if the project is abandoned – for example where a high level of advertizing expenditure has been incurred in advance.)

60. Review your pricing structure.
You may need to review your pricing structure in the light of these calculations. Remember that whatever your costs you cannot charge more than the marketplace will bear. Make sure this gives you an adequate return. Decide on any discounting criteria you will use (e.g. for bulk purchases or prompt payment). Will your price/ quality specification be consistent with your special niche in the marketplace?

61. Draw up a specification for your location and premises.

Set out the criteria which will enable you to judge whether the location and nature of the premises required for your business is appropriate. What will you use your premises for? Will it be helpful for your factory to be near your suppliers – or customers? Should your shop be among other similar shops (e.g. antiques) or distanced from competitors? Should your premises be readily accessible to personal callers – or is all your selling done by telephone, correspondence and visits to customers' premises?

Where will the business be situated? Can you get the appropriate planning permission? Do the likely costs fit your business plans so far? Have you taken fully into account likely rent reviews and changes in business rates?

What accommodation, services (electricity, gas, water, drainage, telephone lines, high speed Internet access etc.) will you need? What vehicles will need to visit your premises, either for parking or to unload equipment and materials? How many people will you employ, where will they work, what facilities will they need to attract and retain them? Will the premises be rented, leased, purchased? Many technical matters are generally involved and you would be wise to seek advice. Set out these points on paper.

62. Set out your sales forecast and sales targets.

You must now take your earlier rough estimates and decide on the figures you will use for detailed calculations on a month-by-month basis for the first year, and on a quarter-by-quarter basis for the next two years. It may sound impossible to make such detailed forecasts, but without these you do not have a business plan. It is unlikely that your forecasts will be achieved to the letter,

Figure 11. Sales Forecasts

		Item 1	Item 2	Item 3	Item 4	Item 5
Price/unit						
	month	SALES IN UNITS				
Year 1	1					
	2					
	3					
	4					
	5					
	6					
	7					
	8					
	9					
	10					
	11					
	12					
	quarter					
Year 2	1					
	2					
	3					
	4					
Year 3	1					
	2					
	3					
	4					

but they are vital for planning and, later, for monitoring your business performance. Once you have written down your best attempts at sales forecasting, these figures become your sales targets. Use a table based on Figure 11 to record your results.

63. Forecast your sales revenue.

This is simply a matter of bringing together your sales forecasts with your pricing policy over the three-year period. There are two ways of dealing with inflation. One is to create the plan at current prices, i.e. ignoring inflation altogether. When you update and carry forward the plan next year you can then use next year's costs and prices. Alternatively, you can estimate what cost increases you expect and what adjustment you will make to your prices in years 2 and 3 of the plan. When forecasting sales revenue you must take into account the time taken for customers to pay. The total sales volume in a period is used to calculate income generated and the profit/loss, but the revenue (i.e. the cash flowing into the business) depends on how quickly people pay. Be careful to specify when you expect cash to actually arrive in your bank account. Use Figure 12 as a guide to how to write down your estimates.

64. Firm up your advertizing strategy.

Having decided earlier how you will reach your customers and evoke a response, you must now go into more detail on the costs involved, when you will place advertisements, organize leaflet drops or mail shots, the Internet and so forth. Make a note of when payments will be required for your advertizing efforts on a month-by-month basis for year one, and quarterly thereafter. If you intend to advertise by taking stands at trade fairs, show the costs as and when they will occur.

Figure 12. Sales Revenue Forecasts						
	month	Item A	Item B	Item C	Item D	Item E
Year 1	1					
	2					
	3					
	4					
	5					
	6					
	7					
	8					
	9					
	10					
	11					
	12					
	quarter					
Year 2	1					
	2					
	3					
	4					
Year 3	1					
	2					
	3					
	4					

65. Describe how you will convert responses into sales.
Who will sell your products and services? What methods will they use to 'close the sale'? What support activity will be carried out – packing and sending out goods, recording sales and returns, preparing delivery notes, invoices and credit notes, answering queries etc. Outline any such activities and show how the costs will be met. An old adage is worth repeating – a sale is only completed when you have the money!

66. Prepare your credit control for sales.
If you sell goods or services on credit terms you will need to institute a system for monitoring payments and following up unpaid bills. Again record this and any associated costs. If you decide to use factoring this may improve your cash flow – but at a cost to your profitability which you will need to take into account in your pricing policy.

PART VI

Essential calculations

- Now you must start on some serious sums.
- Estimate your requirements for capital items and cash.
- Estimate your fixed and variable costs.
- Prepare your profit/loss and cash flow forecasts.

67. Estimate capital expenditure costs.

What will you need to buy and when? What will each item cost, and how long will it last? You will need this information for both cash flow and profit/loss calculations, to estimate your cash requirements and to draw up your balance sheets. See Figure 13. This table assumes that you will purchase individual items. If you intend to lease or hire capital items they must be included in your general overhead expenditure. Include any premium payments on premises and similar items, e.g. deposits for items to be obtained by hire purchase agreements.

The date when a replacement is required may not enter into your first three-year plan, but you will need this for later plans as you will need to allow for the expenditure in your longer-term cash flow forecasts and investment strategy.

Figure 13. Capital Expenditure

Capital item	Initial cost	Anticipated purchase date	Anticipated life in years	Date replacement will be required

68. Calculate depreciation on capital items.

Decide on your depreciation policy on items of different kinds (e.g. buildings, fixtures and fittings, manufacturing plant, computers, other equipment, vehicles). You must decide on the useful life of each capital item, and whether you wish to depreciate this by the straight-line or reducing balance method (see Section 77). Use these figures for the draft balance sheets and profit calculations. You will need to talk to your accountant about how these figures are calculated for reporting purposes (e.g. for Company returns or tax returns), but here we are concerned with forecasting for planning purposes, and you should make realistic estimates of how long capital items will be useful.

69. Estimate your fixed costs.

Fixed costs are those costs which, within limits, do not vary with the volume of your sales. Those items of expenditure which vary directly according to how much you sell are called variable costs. Most items of expenditure can be classified as one or the other, but there are some items which are semi-variable. Another complication is that at a certain level of sales you will need to increase the overhead costs, e.g. to obtain more accommodation, staff or machinery.

List all items of fixed costs expenditure and when the cash must be paid. Include the depreciation on capital items from above (**not**, of course, the capital costs), but exclude here any items of expenditure that are dependent on sales – e.g. stock replenishment. Use Figure 14 as a checklist, adding any items peculiar to your business.

For each of the items in this table you will need to estimate the anticipated annual expenditure incurred for the purposes of calculating profit/loss. Incurred is the key word as far as the profit/loss is concerned – whether

Figure 14. Fixed Costs			
	Year 1	Year 2	Year 3
Employees' Salaries and Wages			
Employers' National Insurance			
Training of Staff			
Rent (Rented premises)			
Rates and Water Rates			
Fuel (Gas, Electricity, etc.)			
Telecommunications (incl. Internet)			
Computing Costs			
Postage			
Printing and Stationery			
Subscriptions and Periodicals			
Advertizing and Promotions			
Repairs and Maintenance			
Insurance Payments			
Professional Fees			
Interest Payments			
Bank Charges			
Vehicle and Travel Costs (other than (depreciation and running costs)			
Depreciation – Vehicle			
Depreciation – Other Assets			
Other Expenses (specify)			
TOTAL OVERHEADS			

or not payment is made in that year. When you come to consider your accounting procedures, methods must be used to take into account payments made before or after the year, but which relate to expenditure incurred (or income generated) in that year.

For the purposes of estimating cash flow you will need to determine when the cash has to be paid. In the case of depreciation, of course, no cash is paid at all – although there may be payments associated with the purchase or sale of assets, or interest payments on loans taken out.

70. Estimate variable costs.

Based on your projected sales and the nature of your business, see which costs will be variable, i.e. those which will vary directly as a result of sales. Estimate these variable costs, and when payment will be due. For example, if your variable costs are simply finished goods that you buy in to replace those which are sold, the original cost of the items which have been sold will be the variable costs for profit/loss calculations.

When you come to calculate cash flow, however, you will need to record the cost of such items as and when the expenditure is incurred, irrespective of whether or not these items have been sold, or whether or not they are replacements for items sold.

71. Estimating wages and salaries.

If the wages and salaries relate to permanent employees paid regularly each week or month, then labour costs are effectively fixed. For cash flow purposes the income tax and National Insurance deducted is normally paid to the authorities the following month. Where a portion of the labour costs are dependent on sales volume this may be a variable cost (e.g. if it is a sales-related bonus) or semi-variable (e.g. overtime pay incurred when there is more work). If you take on temporary or seasonal employees because of anticipated extra sales volume these are also variable costs although the relationship between costs and sales may not be straightforward. Care will be required in both estimating and in accounting for such expenditure.

72. Estimating telecommunications and postage costs.

In some businesses these costs may be related to sales volume. In most cases, however, it is difficult to estimate these accurately, but in such cases they may not be major cost factors so that accuracy is not important in preliminary estimates. If the costs are to be large, e.g. if you expect a lot of overseas trade, you will need to do a rough estimate of telephone usage and anticipated mailings. Include here the costs of facsimile transmissions or on-line computer information or communication systems.

73. Rent, business and water rates.

Do you anticipate that leased or rented premises will be required? When will rents be payable (in advance or in arrears, monthly, quarterly or annually)? What will be the annual rent payable? Insert this figure in your fixed costs. How long is the contract? When is a rent increase negotiable? If this falls in your first three years it must be reflected in your figures. Will a premium be required? The cost of this must be spread over the contract period and included in the overhead figure for the profit/loss calculation. The time at which the premium must be paid and when the rent payments fall due should be noted for the cash flow.

What are the anticipated annual business rate charges? How can payment be phased? How do you intend to pay? What will be the annual water rate charges? How can payment be phased? How do you intend to pay?

74. Estimate insurance costs.
List all the kinds of insurance you will need for the business. What annual amount is required? Use for the profit/loss estimates. When will this be paid? Use these figures for cash flow forecasting. You may find Figure 15 helpful.

75. Interest and loan repayments.
Include all interest payable on loans and finance obtained for the business, e.g. property mortgages, bank loans, overdrafts – but exclude vehicles if they are entered separately. It is necessary to separate out repayment of capital from interest payments. See Figure 16.

76. Vehicle and travel costs.
Where the use of the vehicle is not related to the volume of sales, the total annual costs, based on your anticipated mileage (but not depreciation, which is usually entered separately), should be entered in the vehicle expenses section of the fixed costs. Where the use of the vehicle is directly related to volume of sales then you may need to allocate some of the expenditure (e.g. fuel consumption, or a proportion of total expenditure) to variable costs.

77. Depreciation.
There are two common methods used for calculating depreciation, the reducing balance method (e.g. commonly used for vehicles) and the straight-line method. In the reducing balance method the depreciation is calculated as a percentage of the original cost price in the first

Figure 15. Insurance Costs

Type of Insurance	Cover Required	Annual Premium	Payment Dates

Figure 16. Interest and Loan Repayments

Type of loan	Amount	Period	Interest on loan	Annual repayment		Annual interest payable	Monthly or quarterly
				Rate %	Capital		
		TOTALS					

year. Thus a vehicle costing £10,000 might be depreciated at 25% per annum, i.e. depreciation would be £2,500. The new 'book value' of this vehicle at the end of the year becomes £7,500 and the next year's depreciation is based on this, i.e. 25% of £7,500 = £1,875 and so on.

In the straight-line method the life of the item (e.g. a piece of equipment) is estimated (e.g. 5 years) and if it has an estimated residual value (say £200) at that time, depreciation is calculated by taking the original cost (say £10,000) less the residual value and spreading this over the useful life, i.e. in the case of our example, (£10,000 − £200) ÷ 5 = £1,960 per annum. You may find it helpful to draw up a table based on Figure 17 for items costing more than say £250 each.

78. List the sources of finance available.

What will the investors put into your business? Estimate the effect of expenditure on capital items on your liquidity. (Liquidity is the money you actually have available to pay bills with!) Will you need extra funds? If necessary explore alternatives to outright purchase. Consider alternative loan and equity financing arrangements if you will need these. You may need to revise these estimates again if an adverse cash flow situation is predicted when you do detailed calculations.

If other people or organizations have invested in your business, this effectively dilutes the equity. It might also reduce your control over the business as equity holders often expect to have a say in the way you conduct your operation.

The ratio of money that is borrowed by a business to the money invested (equity) is called gearing. Thus if the amount of money provided by lenders is equal to the amount put in by investors the gearing is one. You

Capital item	Initial cost	Final value	Anticipated purchase date	Expected life (in years)	Depreciation per annum	Method

Figure 17. Depreciation

should think twice before exceeding this ratio. Borrowing too much money has been the downfall of more than one business. In a potentially successful business it is tempting to borrow money to become a more highly geared business because if there is an operating profit well above the interest rate, this can lead to higher profits for those who own the equity. This is fraught with danger however; if the anticipated success is not forthcoming the results can be fatal to the business.

79. Plan your capital investment strategy.

Set out how you intend to finance the capital outlay required to run the business. We now need to know, in detail, when you will plan for cash to be injected into the business, and when payments will need to be made for capital items, to maintain cash flow and to service loans with interest and repayments. As before, we need to know this on a month-by-month basis for the first year and on a quarter-by-quarter basis for the next two years. In later years you may be able to fund capital investment from retained profits. A simple table you can use is presented in Figure 18. A key question to consider is how soon this investment will repay the business by the extra speed or capacity it brings.

80. Revise your profit forecast.

You now have the information required to do some preliminary estimates of your profits – or losses – over your early trading periods, the first three years. The results will only be as good as your estimates to date, and there is still work to do to refine these figures, but you will get a first indication of the financial soundness of the planned business. Use the Profit/Loss table in Part X.

Carry out some simple sums which will show you what will happen to your profits if things don't go

Figure 18. Capital Investment

Capital item	Initial cost	Anticipated life in years	Anticipated purchase date	Method of payment	Completion of loan or end of lease

according to plan. For example, if your sales fall short, your opening is delayed, costs rise or your sales are excessive. You now have a much better set of figures to use in the risk calculations described earlier.

81. Decide on how much stock to hold.

You can't afford to run out of key materials, but raw materials, intermediate products or finished goods in storage represent cash that is lying idle, so you will need to think carefully about the levels you will keep and the time it will take to replenish these stocks. You may find Figure 19 helpful. You may need separate tables for different kinds of raw materials, intermediates and finished goods.

In deciding how much work-in-progress and finished goods to hold there are many factors to be taken into account, depending on the business. You will need certain levels of finished goods and work in progress to maintain sales, but at the same time, as with raw materials, holding stocks costs money. You need to set out your proposals, but be prepared to change these in the light of experience. One of the key factors is how long it takes to convert raw materials into finished goods, and how much 'value added' this involves.

Finally estimate the financial implications of your chosen stock levels. Calculate the capital employed in maintaining the raw materials, work in progress and finished goods you intend to hold. Note when payments will fall due for stock replenishment.

82. Forecast cash receipts and payments.

You have earlier forecast receipts from sales, and decided when cash injections will be needed from investors and from lenders. Are there any other anticipated sources of revenue, e.g. asset sales or interest on

Figure 19. Raw Material Stock Levels

Item	Stock levels (minimum)		Stock levels (average)		Re-order policy		
	Quantity	Value (£)	Quantity	Value (£)	Frequency	Quantity	Value (£)

Total average value of raw material stocks held = £ _____

bank deposits? As the next step in calculating cash flow, put these factors together in the appropriate section of the cash flow forecast – see Figure 20.

Set out all anticipated outgoings, including capital items, taxation, National Insurance and value added tax. The timing of these payments is now crucial. These figures should be entered in the next section of the cash flow forecast – Figure 20.

83. Work out the cash flow forecast.
From the figures you have entered you can now see the cash requirements from month to month in the first year – and quarter-by-quarter in the second and third year. From this you can check how much working capital you will need, and when you will need it. Cash remaining at the end of month 1 is added to receipts minus payments for month 2 to give the cash remaining at the end of month 2.

Make provision for the cash you will need ahead of time, and be sure, when you start trading, to monitor cash flow on a monthly basis against your forecasts. Decide on whether you will need to inject more cash or to take out a loan, or request overdraft facilities to cover any possible problems with working capital.

Using all the information now to hand, including any adjustments following your study of the figures (e.g. any overdraft facilities or extra cash injections) to produce a fully revised cash flow forecast.

84. Revise your profit forecasts.
Using figures consistent with your revised cash flow forecast, revise your estimates of profit/loss for each of the first three years. You must now take into account any new factors arising from your study of cash flow or your stockholding requirements – e.g. the possible

Figure 20a. CASH FLOW FORECAST

month =	1	2	3	4	5	6	7	8	9	10	11	12	Total
RECEIPTS													
Opening Balance (B)													
Owner's Investment													
Loans from . . .													
Cash Sales													
Credit Sales													
Asset Disposals													
Interest Received													
TOTAL RECEIPTS (R)													
PAYMENTS													
List here all the payment headings and indicate when you consider payment will fall due.													
TOTAL PAYMENTS (P)													
Calculate and enter here, month-by-month: RECEIPTS LESS PAYMENTS FOR THE MONTH (M)													
Calculate and enter here, month-by-month: CASH REMAINING IN THE BUSINESS (C)													

requirement of an overdraft or loan to cover cash requirements indicated in the cash flow, or to fund your stockholding. Overdrafts and loans involve interest payments which will reduce your profit level. These interest payments must be incorporated in the fixed cost in your profit forecasts.

85. Prepare balance sheets.

Set out the assets and liabilities at the beginning of the trading period for which you are planning. If you are starting the business from scratch, you may find it useful to employ the first column of the cash flow forecast as a 'setting up' column rather than a record of the first month's trading. You can use it to show where the start-up funds are coming from, and what any money has been spent on before the business actually starts to trade. This would provide a useful basis for the opening balance sheet.

Draw up a balance sheet for the end of each year in the planning period (See Figure 21). This should indicate retained profits and also take into account how quickly you expect to pay bills, and to be paid, as well as depreciation and any capital injections or repayments.

Figure 21 – Balance Sheet

LIABILITIES	ASSETS
Capital (owners')	**Fixed Assets**
Owner's investment	Buildings
Retained profit	Plant
	Furniture
	Vehicles
	Computers
Deferred Liability	**Current Assets**
Term loan	Raw materials
	Finished goods
	Debtors
	Cash
Current Liability	
Creditors	
Tax liability	
Bank overdraft	

PART VII

Planning to manage

- Now review the key feature of your plan.
- Think through how you will manage the business.
- Prepare an action plan to implement your business development.
- Plan to monitor your business and to keep proper records.
- Prepare to manage people and relationships effectively.

86. Finalize your business name and address.
This is not as easy as it seems. Most people will want a name that is easy to remember, and may indicate the kind of goods or services on offer. You will need to check that nobody else is using that name – especially anyone near where you will operate from. In the case of a limited company this will be checked anyway. Make sure the name conveys the right 'image' consistent with your proposed market niche. Avoid names that lead to misunderstanding. Bear in mind that your business name may appear in Internet search engines, and you may want to use it in your web and email addresses.

You may well trade from your business location – and this will be your business address. This will appear in your promotional material. Again – does it project the right image? If not, you may need to consider an accommodation address.

87. Review key features of the business plan.
Review any **Special Factors** – licences, patents, copyright, trade marks, insurance, planning permits, qualifications required for specific tasks etc. Now is the time for that final check on the business as you now see it and to consider any action you may need to take over such matters.

Bring out your draft **Nature of the Business** statement. Does it still ring true? Or does it need to be changed in the light of any decisions you have made so far? Have you modified the potential customers you are aiming to do business with? Have you modified your ideas on the goods and services you will offer, or the prices, or the conditions of sale?

Review your **Marketing and Sales** plans. The results of you cash flow forecasts or the profit/loss forecasts may have led you to modify the marketing and sales plans. Make sure that the text you have drafted for your plan is up-to-date.

Review your **People** plans. Earlier on you looked at the skills and knowledge you and your team required, and also the help you would seek from outside. In the light of the way your business has developed, re-visit these assessments and make a note of any necessary changes.

Check for **Financial Consistency**. This is one of the most important set of checks you must carry out. Compare your key financial documents – the sales forecasts, cash flow forecast, the profit/loss forecasts, the opening and closing balance sheets, the capital acquisition sheets, the stockholding sheets and any others you have prepared. Are they consistent? Take sales for example. Are the forecast figures carried through correctly into revenue, stock replacements, variable costs and income for profit calculations? Take a capital item. Is the cash there to purchase it when required, is the proposed purchase recorded, and the depreciation taken into account in the profit/loss and the balance sheets?

88. Plan to manage the business.

If your business is to survive profitably there are a number of important parameters you need to manage and to monitor. You will need to ensure, for example, that your sales performance matches your targets, that your fixed costs are contained within your estimates, that credit control on your sales is tight. Many of these parameters can be monitored by adapting the data in your sales and cash flow forecasts. You will also need to motivate, manage and reward any people who work for you. At the end of the day your business success depends crucially on your personal performance and that of the people who work with you.

You will certainly need to set up proper **Record Systems** so that you can satisfy the requirements of the authorities – e.g. for income tax and National Insurance, value added tax, Companies House returns, and probably some in connection with health and safety matters.

89. Prepare your action plan.

Now you need to map out how you will set about putting your business plan into effect. The technique suggested for this is a very simple version of 'critical path analysis'. This technique will help to ensure that your implementation runs on time. Set out each of the steps you will need to take to make progress. Make a special note of any actions which must be completed before others can begin, e.g. you must arrange a loan before purchasing an asset with the money, you need to obtain planning permission before committing yourself to purchasing a property with a specific use in mind. Make an estimate of how long each activity will take. Draw out a simple diagram of the steps: see the illustration in Figure 22. You will see that the longest 'pathway' from start to finish represents, in fact, the shortest time within which the operation can be achieved. This 'shortest' route is called the critical path because any event on that path that takes longer than expected will, in fact, delay the whole operation. Every event on this path is 'critical'.

90. Plan to monitor your business.

Set out your plans to **Monitor Sales**. One way to do this is to set out your targets for each product or service, allocated for each month. Then record actual sales against these figures. See Figure 23. If your sales targets can be divided into parts and allocated by region or salesperson, you will need a separate table for each part and a summary table. You will need to set up an effective system to collect this information and to collate it on a monthly basis. This will need to be linked firmly to your system for monitoring sales receipts.

Set out your plans to monitor **Income Received**. Your cash flow forecast lists at the top the income anticipated on a month-by-month basis. As with the sales forecast you can prepare a simple table setting out these figures, and alongside space to insert what actually happens. In this case there is merit in adding up what you expect on a cumulative basis as well. See Figure 24 for some ideas on how to set this out. Adapt these for your own purposes.

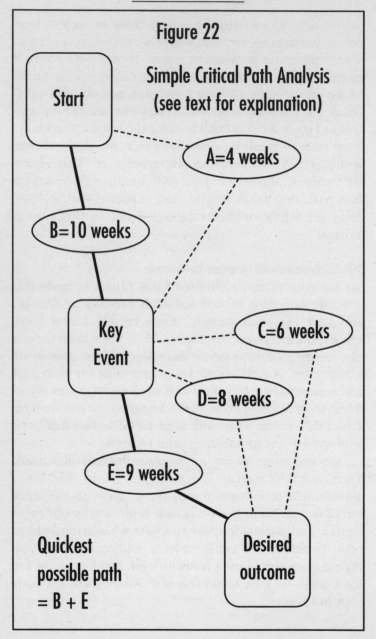

Figure 22

Simple Critical Path Analysis
(see text for explanation)

Start

A=4 weeks

B=10 weeks

Key Event

C=6 weeks

D=8 weeks

E=9 weeks

Desired outcome

Quickest possible path = B + E

Figure 23. Monitoring Sales				
	Month 1		Month 2		etc.
	Forecast	Actual	Forecast	Actual	
SALES					
Number of units of 'A'					
Price of 'A'					
Income from 'A'					
Number of units of 'B'					
Price of 'B'					
Income from 'B'					
Number of units of 'C'					
Price of 'C'					
Income from 'C'					
GROSS INCOME					
RECEIPTS					
Cash sales					
Credit sales					
TOTAL SALES RECEIPTS					

Figure 24. Monitoring Receipts					
	Month 1		Month 2		etc.
	Forecast for month	Actual for month	Forecast to date	Actual to date	
RECEIPTS					
Cash sales					
Credit sales					
TOTAL SALES RECEIPTS					
Investor's cash					
Loan					
Asset disposal					
Interest received					
OTHER RECEIPTS					
TOTAL RECEIPTS					

Set out your plans to monitor **Cash Flow**. You will need to monitor expenditure in the same way as income. A simple, but cumbersome method is to use the cash flow forecast but with two columns for each month (or quarter) for the forecast and actual expenditure for each item of receipt or payment. For expenditure purpose it may be simpler to have a set of budget figures for each month, taken from the cash flow, and to set the actual expenditures against these.

Set out your plans to maintain **Financial Records**. In a very small business a manual system involving working sheets ruled for cash analysis will suffice, but more elaborate businesses need more complex recording systems: for those who have access to computers, there are now straightforward software systems available. State how you will manage these matters.

Set out your plans to monitor the **Marketplace**. You should have done your market analysis by now, studying your prospective customers, the competition and the business environment. However, this is not a once-for-all activity. The world does not stand still. How will you keep abreast of developments?

91. Plan to manage people.

Set out your plans to **recruit, develop, train and motivate** the people who will work with and for your business. Incidentally – the cost of recruitment and training has been included in your estimates, has it not?

PART VIII

Collating the plan

- Check through each section of the plan.
- Make sure the data you will include in your plan is consistent with all the back-up sheets you have used for calculations.
- Complete each section of the plan and assemble them in the recommended order.
- Ensure that you have made any changes required if new information has come to light.

92. Check and complete each section.

Use Figure 25 as your checklist to see that you have each part of the plan ready to assemble into the finished document. Assemble the plan, section by section, carrying out the checks indicated in the table.

The most important question of all is, will the decision-makers (Section 9) be satisfied?

Now you can put the finishing touches to each section of the plan and put it together into one coherent document.

93. Business name and address.

Are you now satisfied with the chosen business name? Is it short, memorable and likely to enhance your business?

Review the criteria for the location of your premises, and all the related factors such as planning permission. Remember that the business address should project an appropriate image of the business and it need not be the same as the location of your operation.

94. Nature of the business.
Does this identify your business idea succinctly? Does it identify the particular customers you are seeking to attract, and identify that unique selling point that will convince them they should come to you for the goods and services described?

95. People in the business.
The essential point of this section is to list out the abilities and experience that you and your colleagues will bring to the business to ensure its success – and to explain how any extra expertise required will be brought in. It is also useful to explain here any steps you intend to take to enhance the skills of yourself or your people – e.g. through training or a programme of study visits. You can use this section to outline any steps you must take regarding health and safety, food hygiene and related matters. Consider how you will cope with the diversity of people you will encounter in your business dealings.

96. Marketing and sales.
Here you should explain the basis of your marketing strategy. What is your knowledge of the marketplace based on? What information do you have about your potential customers, their numbers, their buying habits, their likely uptake of your goods and services? What information do you have about your competitors and any new developments in that area? What steps will you take to maintain market intelligence?

Have you made clear what methods you will use to reach your customers, what response you expect, and how you will convert that response into firm purchases? Are the response rates realistic? Check over the sales forecast figures and how these convert into income received. Will your customers really pay that quickly?

97. Profit and loss forecast.

This should cover three years: it is your final opportunity to spot any inconsistencies or errors. Do check through methodically and wherever possible do cross checks. Arithmetic errors are commonplace and they must all be weeded out now. Check your figures against sales forecasts. Check them against the draft cash flow forecasts. Are they consistent with the balance sheets? Have you carried out the risk assessments – and is the level of risk acceptable if receipts are late, or raw material costs or interest rates rise or whatever is your dominant risk factor?

You should also make clear any assumptions you have made in drawing up these figures.

98. Cash flow forecast.

You should have completed this section, and as with the profit/loss forecast you must now ensure that it is correct and consistent with other sections. A full month-by-month forecast is required for the first year, and quarter-by-quarter for years 2 and 3. Provide notes to explain any figures that are not obvious by inspection.

A particular point to watch is the phasing of receipts from sales and demands for payments. In many ways this is the most crucial part of your plan. A business can survive without profit for a period – but it cannot survive an inability to pay bills.

Figure 25. Outline Business Plan – Expanded

	Key Questions
NAME OF THE BUSINESS	Does this fit the nature of the business you have planned?
ADDRESS OF THE BUSINESS	Does this address project the right image? Are the premises suitable for the purpose?
NATURE OF THE BUSINESS	Does this statement match with your current thinking? Is it clear and unambiguous?
PEOPLE IN THE BUSINESS HEALTH AND SAFETY	Have you identified the key skills needed for success and how you will ensure these are available to the business? Have you a clear policy on health and safety and on employing people? Have you a clear policy for dealing with the potential diversity of people that form your customers, business contacts and, if appropriate, employees?
COMMUNICATIONS STRATEGY	How will you communicate with customers, suppliers and business contacts and colleagues? How will you gather business data for ongoing planning and decision-making?

Figure 25a. Outline Business Plan – Expanded (continued)	
	Key Questions (continued)
MARKETING AND SALES STRATEGY	Is this consistent with your 'nature of the business' statement? Are you certain that you have correctly identified potential customers, and products and services they will buy from you – at your quality and prices?
PROFIT AND LOSS FORECASTS	Are these forecasts complete, healthy, realistic and based on your most current assumptions?
CASH FLOW FORECASTS	Have you identified all sources of income and items of expenditure, and when they will occur? Have you made provision to meet payments when they fall due?
CAPITAL EXPENDITURE PLANS	Have you identified all items of capital expenditure and how you will fund them?
STOCK PURCHASING POLICY	Have you decided upon the level of stock to keep, how much you will start with, and in what quantities you will reorder?

Figure 25b. Outline Business Plan – Expanded (continued)	
	Key Questions (continued)
FUNDS REQUIRED – FINANCIAL BASE	Are you satisfied that you have a sound financial base? Have you confirmed the sources and application of the funds you will require?
MANAGEMENT INFORMATION	Have you clearly set out how you intend to monitor key aspects of the business as it runs and what methods you will use for recording financial and other important data?
SPECIAL FACTORS including the ENVIRONMENT	Are you confident that you have identified all the special factors relating to your business, and made appropriate arrangements to satisfy these? What actions will you plan regarding environmental factors?
ACTION PLAN	Does this clearly set out the key actions and decisions that need to be taken and the target dates for each step?

99. Capital expenditure.

It is often helpful to include a simple table, as illustrated earlier, listing the capital items you will require, how much each will cost, when you expect to purchase each item and the method of payment envisaged. You will also need to indicate the useful life of the item and how you will take account of depreciation on different categories.

100. Stock purchasing and stock control.

If appropriate, complete this section as indicated previously, including any notes you consider necessary to explain your policy.

101. Funds required and financial base.

List here the sources of funds in the business and how these will be applied to capital expenditures and working capital. This information must be consistent with your cash flow forecast, profit /loss forecast and balance sheets. Check on your gearing – Section 78.

102. Management information.

There is no need for a great deal of detail in your written business plan. Summarize the key points of the monitoring and recording systems you will use. Keep the notes you used to prepare this section as they will form the guidelines for yourself and your managers in the future.

103. Special factors including the environment.

Summarize the special factors which relate to your business, and how you intend to satisfy each requirement. From earlier sections you will recall that these factors may include items such as licences, planning permits and qualified people (for certain activities). Environmental factors will depend on the nature of your operation: take into account the impact of any relevant legislation, rules or normal practices in your industrial sector.

104. Action plan.

The action plan you prepared to implement your business plan should now be finally revised and updated in the light of any new developments.

PART IX

Implementation

- Complete your checklists on management, marketing and money.
- Implement your plan.
- Deal with any variations that you had not foreseen.
- Be prepared to update the plan in due course.

105. Conduct your final viability check.
The following checklists amplify those provided in Part IV. Go though the lists to satisfy yourself that every angle has been covered. These lists have been adapted from *The 24-Hour Business Plan*.

106. Management checklist – the men and women involved.
- Do you and your management team have the motivation to see you through the hard times, the long hours and the frustrations of running this business?
- Do you and your management team have the technical skills to make the products and to provide the services you envisage?
- Do you and your management team have all the skills needed to look after the administrative side of the business, including all the money matters?

- Has your organization the ability to sell your goods/ services to the potential customers you have identified?
- Are you prepared to modify your business plans in the light of what people will want to buy?
- Are you confident that you and your key managers will be able to manage skills and time to full effect?
- Have you made arrangements to plug any gaps in the expertise of your team? How do you plan to ensure that they are kept up-to-date?
- Will you be able to get all the skilled workers you need in the location(s) you have chosen for your business?
- Are working conditions, wages and other rewards adequate to attract and retain the staff you will need?
- Is there adequate transport available to enable your workforce to attend work regularly and punctually?
- Are there any special requirements related to qualified people (e.g. divers, HGV drivers, transport managers, registered traders) in your business, and are you sure you can attract and retain such people?
- Have you decided what arrangements to make, if any, concerning pension arrangements for your staff?
- Have you taken steps to ensure that you can cope effectively with the diversity of people with whom you will be dealing on a day to day basis?
- Have you taken full account of health and safety matters?

107. Marketing and sales checklist.
- What is so special about the product that you intend to sell or the service that you intend to provide?
- How do you know that anyone will want to buy them?

- How much will you charge for your products or services? Will people be prepared to pay those prices?
- Are you sure that you can provide those goods or services at these prices, make a profit and manage cash flow?
- Why should anyone buy your goods or services rather than others on the market?
- Why should they buy products and services from you and not from your competitors?
- Is this the right time to start providing the goods or services that you have in mind? Is this the moment when people will want them?
- Will you be able to develop your product or develop new products as your market develops?
- Have you considered how you will advertise or promote your product and how much this will cost?
- Do you know who your competitors are and what products they are selling?
- Have you spoken to any potential customers about the product or service that you intend to provide?
- Have you planned to make adequate provision for the follow-up of all enquiries from potential customers?
- Have you planned to institute a method of keeping abreast of the needs of your customers and the situation in the marketplace?
- If you intend to use intermediaries (e.g. wholesalers, distributors or agents) are you confident that they will promote your products and services?

108. Money management checklist.
- Will your business make a profit?
- Will you be able to pay each bill when it arrives?
- What financial resources will you need to be successful, especially over the initial trading period?

- Are you fully prepared to make your share of this financial commitment?
- Do you need – can you obtain – a loan at a reasonable rate of interest?
- Are you confident that you can pay back any loans over a reasonable period, and pay the interest?
- Have you researched, listed and estimated the costs that you will incur, and when these expenditures will be required?
- Have you included costs associated with the Internet, health and safety, the environment?
- In particular, have you adequately researched your capital requirements and needs for "working capital"?
- Have you a clear idea of when income will start to flow?
- Have you considered your insurance needs and any licences and permits that will be required?
- What sources of information, help and advice do you need? Do you know where these can be obtained?
- Have you discovered any problems that you have never had to deal with before?
- Have you made adequate provision for depreciation and for the rapid obsolescence of some kinds of equipment?
- Have you taken into account the sudden and dramatic rise in rent that might occur at rent review time?
- Have you built a sound relationship with your accountant and bank manager?

109. Location checklist.
- Are your chosen locations and buildings suitable for your purpose?
- Do your premises have all the services you require, including any special drainage, air extraction or high voltages?

- Are your facilities for manufacture, storage, sales and offices adequate?
- Will your suppliers, customers and delivery vehicles be able to get into and out of your premises, and manoeuvre adequately?
- Are you confident that you have made adequate arrangements for the maintenance of any crucial plant and equipment?
- Are you sure you have adequate supplies of raw materials from reliable sources?
- Can you obtain planning permission as required?

110. Implementing the plan.

You will need to bring together the managers who will need to implement the plan. Give them a copy each to read before you meet. The goals to be set for each manager are implicit in the plan: these need to be made explicit and incorporated into a set of clear month-by-month objectives, linked to the monitoring systems devised. Many organizations find it helpful to draw up regularly monthly reports based on the agreed performance indicators – hopefully within a week of the end of the month.

The Chief Executive or Managing Partner will need to examine these and discuss the results with each manager concerned.

If each department has its own budget, derived from the plan, these monthly results can show actual income and expenditure against the forecast, target figures, or in the case of sales, the actual against expected sales figures and the related payments received.

111. Dealing with deviations.

In practice a business does not generally run to plan. The business plan and the information used to compile the plan form an excellent basis to consider the effect of any deviations – e.g. slow sales, slow sales receipts, changes in raw material prices.

In order to interpret what is happening it is vital to have a note of the assumptions on which the plan is based – what sales were expected – where they would come from – what rate of response was expected from a particular advertizing medium and so forth. It is also worthwhile to bear in mind or to refer to the results of your 'risk analyses'.

This data forms an essential basis for sound decisions in the light of changing circumstances. It is important not to discard the plan and start on cut-backs as a gut reaction to such difficulties. Re-examine your data, your marketplace – and see if there are not alternative sources of supply, or of advertizing, or of customers. Often, the real question is whether you can survive by adapting to the changing market, and here the thorough analysis conducted as a result of your planning, and the updating provided by your market monitoring can be invaluable.

112. Updating business plans.
It is sound practice to update the business plan once a year. This means turning the second year's quarterly figures into monthly ones, taking full account of any changes in the business, and preparing a new set of figures for the fourth year. It is tempting to take all the figures and add a factor to take account of inflation. Don't. Work out each figure afresh, taking into account the results to date, what you know about price changes, and – most important of all – any action you intend to take which might change the figures – e.g. a change in your product mix, a new source of raw material, a tighter control of a particular item of expenditure.

As part of the preparation for this 'rolling forward' of the plan, do not forget to scan the business environment again, considering particularly your competitors. Above all, stay close to your customers, how they are developing, and how their needs are changing.

PART X

Your own plan

In the following pages you will find a 'blank' plan with examples of all the main sections, headings and tables. For a simple business you can simply fill in the blank spaces, but in most cases you will need to adapt the pattern to fit your own requirements.

BUSINESS PLAN

(name of business)

(address of business)

NATURE OF BUSINESS

Describe the nature of the products and services to be provided and outline the customers and mode of promotion and delivery.

KEY PEOPLE

Name the key people – including yourself – who will work in the business and outline the knowledge, skills and experience they will contribute to the success of the enterprise. Indicate if you intend to recruit staff, how many and with what skills. State you policies on health and safety, employing people and diversity

_____

_____

_____

_____

_____

_____

_____

_____

_____

NOTE: Are there any areas of skill and knowledge which are needed in addition to those mentioned above? How will you deal with this, e.g. will you have some training to cover this or sub-contract this work?

COMMUNICATIONS

Outline how you will communicate with customers, suppliers, business contacts and colleagues. Show how you will gather business data for ongoing planning and decision-making.

_____

_____

_____

_____

_____

_____

_____

_____

_____

_____

NOTE: You will need to make clear what use you intend to make of the Internet, periodicals and suchlike.

SALES PLAN

CUSTOMERS
Describe precisely the key decision-makers involved in purchasing your products and services.

_____

_____

_____

_____

_____

_____

PATTERN OF DEMAND
Outline anticipated sales over the first year, and note in particular any anticipated seasonal variation in sales.

_____

_____

_____

_____

_____

_____

_____

SALES PLAN – CONTINUED

PRICING POLICY
Outline the prices to be charged and how these were determined.

_____

_____

_____

_____

_____

_____

REACHING CUSTOMERS
Outline how potential customers will be informed about the products and services, attracted to make enquiries, and encouraged to make purchases.

_____

_____

_____

_____

_____

_____

_____

SALES AND REVENUE FORECAST

MONTH =	1	2	3	4	5	6	7	8	9	10	11	12	Total
SALES													
Income from A §													
Income from B §													
Income from C §													
Gross income generated from sales													
RECEIPTS Cash sales													
Credit sales													
TOTAL SALES RECEIPTS													

§ Income from A = Number of Units A × price of A/unit, etc.
Remember that the projected total sales income generated in the year is used for your profit/loss forecast, but the income received is used for the cash flow forecast.

Profit/loss Forecast			
	Year 1	Year 2	Year 3
SALES FORECAST – revenue generated (Sum of units sold × unit price in each case) = **GROSS TURNOVER**			
Less variable cost incurred in generating these sales . . .			
Gives **GROSS PROFIT**			
Plus any other income . . .			
Gives **TOTAL INCOME**			
Less **OVERHEADS** from below . . .			
Gives **PROFIT/LOSS** before tax.			
OVERHEADS Employees net wages Income tax and NI Training expenses Rent (rented premises) Rates and water rates Fuel (gas, electricity, etc.) Telecommunications Computing Postage Printing and stationery Subscriptions and periodicals Advertizing and promotions Insurance payments Professional fees Loan repayments Bank charges Bank interest Repairs and maintenance Vehicle and travel costs (exclude vehicle purchases) Depreciation – vehicles Depreciation – computer equipment Depreciation – fixtures and fittings Depreciation – plant and machinery Other expenses – specify			
TOTAL OVERHEADS			

NOTE: You will need to ensure that the items you list cover all the income and expenditure

CASH FLOW FORECAST – YEAR ONE

month =	1	2	3	4	5	6	7	8	9	10	11	12	Total
RECEIPTS													
Opening Balance													
Owner's investment													
Loans from . . .													
Cash Sales													
Credit Sales													
Asset Disposals													
Interest received													
TOTAL RECEIPTS													

CASH FLOW FORECAST – YEAR ONE continued

month =	1	2	3	4	5	6	7	8	9	10	11	12	Total
PAYMENTS													
Premium on lease													
Purchase of property													
Puchase of plant													
Furniture and fittings													
Purchase of vehicles													
Raw materials													
Goods for sale													
Employees net wages													
Income tax and NI													
Training expenses													

CASH FLOW FORECAST – YEAR ONE continued

month =	1	2	3	4	5	6	7	8	9	10	11	12	Total
Rent (rented premises)													
Rates and water rates													
Fuel (gas, electricity etc.)													
Telecommunications													
Postage													
Printing & stationery													
Subscriptions & periodicals													
Advertizing & promotions													
Repairs & maintenance													
Vehicle & travel costs (exclude vehicle purchases)													

CASH FLOW FORECAST – YEAR ONE continued

month =	1	2	3	4	5	6	7	8	9	10	11	12	Total
Insurance payments													
Professional fees													
Loan repayments													
Bank charges													
Bank interest													
Value added tax													
Other expenses (specify)													
TOTAL PAYMENTS													
RECEIPTS LESS PAYMENTS FOR THE MONTH													
CASH REMAINING IN THE BUSINESS													

CASH FLOW FORECAST – YEARS TWO AND THREE

Year/Quarter =	2/1	2/2	2/3	2/4	3/1	3/2	3/3	3/4
RECEIPTS								
Opening Balance								
Owner's investment								
Loans from								
Cash Sales								
Credit Sales								
Asset Disposals								
Interest received								
TOTAL RECEIPTS								

CASH FLOW FORECAST – YEARS TWO AND THREE continued

Year/Quarter =	2/1	2/2	2/3	2/4	3/1	3/2	3/3	3/4
PAYMENTS								
Premium on lease								
Purchase of property								
Puchase of plant								
Furniture and fittings								
Purchase of vehicles								
Raw materials								
Goods for sale								
Employees net wages								
Income tax and NI								
Training expenses								

CASH FLOW FORECAST – YEARS TWO AND THREE continued								
Year/Quarter =	2/1	2/2	2/3	2/4	3/1	3/2	3/3	3/4
Rent (rented premises)								
Rates and water rates								
Fuel (gas, electricity etc.)								
Telecommunications								
Postage								
Printing & stationery								
Subscriptions & periodicals								
Advertizing & promotions								
Repairs & maintenance								
Vehicle & travel costs (exclude vehicle purchases)								

CASH FLOW FORECAST – YEARS TWO AND THREE continued

Year/Quarter =	2/1	2/2	2/3	2/4	3/1	3/2	3/3	3/4
Insurance payments								
Professional fees								
Loan repayments								
Bank charges								
Bank interest								
Value added tax								
Other expenses (specify)								
TOTAL PAYMENTS								
RECEIPTS LESS PAYMENTS FOR THE MONTH								
CASH REMAINING IN THE BUSINESS								

CAPITAL EXPENDITURE

Prepare a list of all the capital items costing more than £250 that you will need in the first three years. Include buildings and vehicles. Indicate in each case whether the article will be purchased outright or subject to a loan, rented or leased.

Capital item	Initial cost	Anticipated purchase date	Method of payment	Completion of loan or end of lease

STOCK LEVELS: RAW MATERIALS

Item	Stock Levels (minimum)		Stock Levels (minimum)		Re-Order		
	Quantity	Value (£)	Quantity	Value (£)	Frequency	Quantity	Value (£)

TOTAL average value of raw materials held = _____

STOCK LEVELS: WORK IN PROGRESS

Item	Stock Levels (minimum)		Stock Levels (minimum)	
	Quantity	Value (£)	Quantity	Value (£)

TOTAL average value of raw materials held = _____

STOCK LEVELS: FINISHED GOODS

Item	Stock Levels (minimum)		Stock Levels (minimum)		Re-Order (if appropriate – e.g. if these are goods bought in for resale)		
	Quantity	Value (£)	Quantity	Value (£)	Frequency	Quantity	Value (£)

TOTAL average value of raw materials held = _____

FINANCIAL BASE

Note below how the company will be funded, and any loans or overdrafts that may be required: you may find it helpful to present opening and closing balance sheets using the following pages.

_____

_____

_____

_____

_____

_____

_____

_____

_____

_____

_____

_____

MANAGEMENT INFORMATION SYSTEMS

Outline in note form how you intend to maintain financial and other quantitative records.

OPENING BALANCE SHEET
(start of year)

LIABILITIES		ASSETS	
Capital (owner's)		**Fixed Assets**	
Owner's investment	_____	Buildings	_____
Retained profit	_____	Plant	_____
	_____	Furniture	_____
		Vehicles	_____
		Computers	_____
			_____
Deferred Liability		**Current Assets**	
Term loan	_____	Raw materials	_____
	_____	Finished goods	_____
		Debtors	_____
		Cash	_____
			_____
Current Liability			
Creditors	_____		
Tax liability	_____		
Bank overdraft	_____		
	_____		

CLOSING BALANCE SHEET
(end of year)

LIABILITIES		ASSETS	
Capital (owner's)		**Fixed Assets**	
Owner's investment	_____	Buildings	_____
Retained profit	_____	Plant	_____
	_____	Furniture	_____
		Vehicles	_____
		Computers	_____
			_____
Deferred Liability		**Current Assets**	
Term loan	_____	Raw materials	_____
	_____	Finished goods	_____
		Debtors	_____
		Cash	_____
			_____
Current Liability			
Creditors	_____		
Tax liability	_____		
Bank overdraft	_____		
	_____		

SPECIAL FACTORS

List here any special factors to be borne in mind – e.g. licences, permits, planning permission, etc. to be obtained. Indicate any special **insurances** required and actions that must be taken to cope with environmental factors.

_____

_____

_____

_____

_____

_____

_____

_____

_____

_____

_____

_____

_____

_____

ACTION PLAN

When do you plan to take fresh initiatives based on your plan? List key decisions/actions that need to be taken. Note any instance where more information is needed and how you intend to obtain this.

Decision	Target date	Information needed

FREE PERSONAL TRAINER SESSION

---

with *FitnessFirst*

If you're looking to improve your motivation and need a change to your current gym routine, look no further! Here's the perfect offer to boost your energy levels and give your fitness regime a kick-start!

You can book a free personal trainer session with one of the participating *FitnessFirst* venues. To take up this offer simply cut out the token overleaf and send it with your till receipt and a stamped self-addressed envelope to **Perfect Series Personal Trainer Session offer**, MKM House, Manchester M16 0XX. You will be sent a Personal Trainer voucher plus a list of participating venues. Call the venue closest in your area to arrange a suitable date and time. When calling the venue state that you hold a **Free Personal Trainer Voucher**. You *FitnessFirst* personal trainer will give you a **Free** consultation, and a 1½ hour session focusing on your own personal goals, combined with a free day pass allowing access to the club facilities.

HAPPY TRAINING!

FitnessFirst is also offering a fantastic discount on membership. Save £5 each month when you join as a 'Gold' member for just £29 per month outside of London and £39 per month within London. 'Gold' membership will allow you to use the great facilities at *FitnessFirst* all year round.

All associated joining and administration fees will apply.

If you have any queries or require further information regarding this offer, please call our Helpline on 0161 877 1113. (Lines open Mon-Fri 9am-5.30pm, calls charged at standard rate)

SEE OVER FOR TERMS AND CONDITIONS AND TOKEN

FREE PERSONAL TRAINER SESSION

with *Fitness First*

Get fit with a private consultation from one of *Fitness First*'s specially selected personal trainers

Claim by 31.12.03. Voucher valid until 31.03.04 See below for terms and conditions.

Cash redemption value 0.01p

TERMS AND CONDITIONS

1. Offer open to all residents over 18 in the UK and Republic of Ireland. 2. One **Free Personal Trainer voucher** entitles the bearer to one free session with a personal trainer. The session will take place at the *Fitness First* health club where the participating personal trainer is based. The voucher also entitles the bearer to the use of the fitness and leisure facilities on the day the session is booked. Be aware that facilities differ from club to club, although most venues offer free use of the gym and pool. 3. The discounted membership offer allows customers to save £5 per month when applying for a 'Gold' membership. You can become a Gold member for just £29 per month outside of London and £39 per month within London. All associated joining and administration fees apply. 4. The voucher is valid for use until 31.03.04 Certain date restrictions may apply; these can be verified with the *Fitness First* venue of your choice. 5. Original vouchers only. 6. Your free session has to be booked in advance. 7. The **Personal Trainer voucher** cannot be used in conjunction with any other promotion or offer. 8. One person may book one session with a participating trainer on one occasion only. 9. Standard terms and conditions of personal trainer sessions apply and are available at each *Fitness First* venue. 10. Customers may be required to complete a health and fitness form before beginning training. 11. The Promoter and MKM can accept no liability for personal loss or injury in any session with a personal trainer, as far as permitted by law. 12. The cash redemption value of each voucher is 0.01p, and no alternative will be offered. This promotion is administered on behalf of the promoter Random House, 20 Vauxhall Bridge Road, London, SW1V 2SA by MKM Marketing & Promotions Ltd, Manchester M16 0XX. If you have any queries, or require further information on this offer, please call our HELPLINE on 0161 877 1113. (Lines open from Mon-Fri 9am-5.30pm calls charged at standard rates)